SUMO

SUMO
From Rite to Sport

by P. L. Cuyler

New York · WEATHERHILL · *Tokyo*

Revised and updated by Doreen Simmons. Cover photographs by Joel Sackett.

NOTE: Throughout this book East Asian names are given
in East Asian order, surname preceding given name.

First edition, 1979
First paperback edition, 1985

Published by John Weatherhill, Inc., of New York and Tokyo, with
editorial offices at 7–6–13 Roppongi, Minato-ku, Tokyo 106, Japan.
Protected by copyright under terms of the International Copyright
Union; all rights reserved. Printed and first published in Japan.

Library of Congress Cataloging in Publication Data: Cuyler, Patricia. /
Sumo: from rite to sport. / Bibliography: p. / Includes index. /
1. Sumo. / I. Title. / GV1197.C89 1979 / 796.8′125 / 79–18859 / ISBN
0–8348–0145–0   ISBN 0–8348–0203–1 pbk.

Contents

A Note to the Revised Edition

Since the first publication of this book in 1979, there have been great changes in the world of sumo. Indeed, a book on the subject begins to go out of date as soon as it is printed. The publisher therefore approached me with the task of an updated edition, which would also incorporate corrections and improvements. Since this was only the second book to attempt a comprehensive survey of sumo, there were inevitably errors and omissions, and the publishers had invited six knowledgeable people to submit comments and suggestions. In making this revision, I have carefully considered all of these, as well as the published critiques of the original book. I have also reviewed Japanese sources and gone through the small number of books, booklets, magazines, and articles which have been published in English. These sources, it must be noted, rarely agree among themselves, and the choice of the most solid documentation of a particular fact is frequently a hard one.

The judgment whether to accept or reject suggestions was mine alone. The major part of the book remains unchanged. In the case of modern sumo, a great deal of new writing was required. An attempt to keep the text within the same framework and length while incorporating new material has made rewriting and condensing necessary even when no objection could be raised to the original, and for this I apologize to the author, whose achievement in putting together a book of this scope I do not wish to slight.

Even though the first-time spectator can quickly grasp the basics, sumo is an enormously complicated subject. It is striking, when one reads all the available English-language writing on it, how much divergence there is about what is going on. My own approach to sumo developed at the first tournament I watched, at the old Kuramae Kokugikan in January 1974. I had gone armed with a magazine article that purported to tell me how to recognize the two families of referees by the way in which they held their wooden fans when announcing the contestants: Kimura palm up, Shikimori palm down. At the end of the day, during which I had seen little wrestling, since my eyes had gone from program to referee's hand throughout, I had established beyond a doubt that all the Kimuras but one held their palms down, and all the Shikimoris held their palms up. (Years later I was able to inquire about the odd man out, and was told, "He is an individualist.")

From that day I have continued to read that magazine and anything else written in English about sumo; but I believe nothing until I have seen it for myself and also checked it with a reliable Japanese source. The programs I have collected since 1974—there are over 250 of them now—have all manner of information and reminders jotted in the margins: how many disputed decisions, which judge sat where, which referee fell out of the ring, when the spotlights went on, who was doing the NHK commentary that day, when the foreign sumo writers and commentators arrived in the auditorium, the color and design of a referee's new costume . . . anything that caught this magpie mind.

Although I have done quite an amount of writing on sumo in the past few years, I continue to regard it as a hobby—an absorbing and multifaceted one, to be sure, but still a hobby. To the many who feel the same, this revision is offered.

Doreen Simmons

Ryogoku
January 1985

Introduction

IN THE SPRING OF 1854 Commodore Matthew C. Perry of the United States Navy succeeded in concluding a treaty of trade and friendship with the Japanese shogunate, thus prying open a door to an exotic country that had remained firmly shut against the Western world during almost two and a half centuries of self-imposed isolation. Following the signing of the concessions an elaborate exchange of gifts was made by both sides: the treaty house at the port of Yokohama was crowded with delicate pieces of lacquerware, rich brocades and silks, porcelains, fans, and pipe cases. The Japanese interpreter translated the long list of presents into Dutch, whereupon it was further rendered into English by a member of Perry's crew. As the commodore made ready to depart, the Japanese officials told him that there was still one article intended for the American president that had not yet been exhibited, and they conducted the officers to the beach, where several hundred immense sacks of rice were heaped up, ready to be loaded on board the American ships.

"While contemplating these substantial evidences of Japanese generosity," recorded Francis L. Hawkes, the official chronicler of the Perry expeditions, in his report to the United States Congress two years later, "the attention of all was suddenly riveted upon a body of monstrous fellows, who tramped down the beach like so many huge elephants. They were professional wrestlers, and formed part of the retinue of the princes, who kept them for their private amusement and for public entertainment. They were some twenty-five in number, and were men enormously tall in stature, and immense in weight of flesh. Their scant costume, which was merely a colored cloth about the loins, adorned with fringes and emblazoned with the armorial bearings of the prince to whom each belonged, revealed their gigantic proportions in all the bloated fulness of fat and breadth of muscle."[1]

The princes—the daimyo, or provincial lords—who accompanied their wrestlers set them to removing the 125-pound sacks of rice to a spot closer to the boats as a preliminary exhibition of the wrestlers' strength. The Japanese officials then proposed that the commodore and his party should retire to the treaty house, where they would have an opportunity of seeing the wrestlers exhibit their professional prowess. There the guests found that a circular space some twelve feet in diameter and enclosed by a ring had been laid out in front of the building and divans covered with red cloth arranged for the Japanese commissioners, their attendants, and the Americans. The bands from the ships were sent for and occasionally broke forth during the performance with lively strains of music.

> As soon as the spectators had taken their seats, the naked wrestlers were brought out into the ring, and the whole number, being divided into two opposing parties, tramped heavily backward and forward, looking defiance at each other, but not engaging in any contest, as their object was merely to parade their points, to give the beholders, as it were, an opportunity to form an estimate of their comparative powers, and to make up their betting-books. They soon retired behind some screens placed for the purpose, where all, with the exception of two, were again clothed in full dress and took their position on seats in front of the spectators.
>
> The two who had been reserved out of the band, now, on the signal being given by the heralds, who were seated on opposite sides, presented themselves. They came in, one after the other, from behind the screen, and walked with slow and deliberate steps, as became such huge animals, into the centre of the ring. Then they ranged themselves, one against the other, at a distance of a few yards. They crouched for a while, eyeing each other with a wary look, as if each were watching for a chance to catch his antagonist off his guard. As the spectator looked on these overfed monsters, whose animal natures had been so carefully and

1.   Woodblock print of bulky sumo wrestlers delivering the shogun's gift of bales of rice to the scrawny American sailors who accompanied Admiral Perry to Japan in 1853.

2.   An etching entitled Japanese Gladiators, *by S. Palmer. Published in the* Illustrated Times of London *in 1858.*

successfully developed, and as he watched them, glaring with brutal ferocity at each other, ready to exhibit the cruel instincts of a savage nature, it was easy for him to lose all sense of their being human creatures, and to persuade himself that he was beholding a couple of brute beasts thirsting for one another's blood. They were, in fact, like a pair of fierce bulls, whose nature they had not only acquired, but even in their look and movements.

As they continued to eye each other they stamped the ground heavily, pawing as it were in impatience, and then stooping their huge bodies, they grasped handfuls of dirt and flung it with an angry toss over their backs,' or rubbed it impatiently between their giant palms, or under their stout shoulders. They now crouched low, still keeping their eyes fixed upon each other and watching every movement, until, in an instant, they had both simultaneously heaved their massive forms in opposing force, body to body, with a shock that might have stunned an ox. The equilibrium of their monstrous frames was hardly disturbed by the concussion, the effect of which was but barely visible in the quiver of the hanging flesh of their bodies. As they came together, they had thrown their brawny arms around each other, and were now entwined in a desperate struggle, each striving with all his enormous strength to throw his adversary. Their great muscles rose with the distinct outline of the sculptured form of a colossal Hercules, their bloated countenances swelled up with gushes of blood which seemed ready to burst through the skin of their reddened faces, their huge bodies palpitated with emotion as the struggle continued. At last, one of the antagonists fell, with his immense weight, heavily upon the ground, and being declared vanquished, was assisted to his feet and conducted from the ring. . . . This disgusting exhibition did not terminate until the whole twenty-five had, successively, in pairs, displayed their immense powers and savage qualities. . . .

Acting Master McCauley of the Powhatan wrote of the matches in his diary: "It was a very unsatisfactory trial of strength, there were one or two falls, but, after all, any wrestler that I have heretofore seen of half the muscle would have laughed at them. . . ."[2]

To a mid-nineteenth-century American sailor, who would have been accustomed to his own country's unruly and often bloody affairs known as the public wrestling match, in which no holds were barred and two angry, swearing opponents rolled each other about in the dirt until one finally conceded defeat, Japanese wrestling may have seemed more than a trifle unsatisfying. For, while rich in tradition and symbolism, sumo surely ranks among the simplest and most genteel of all the known combatant sports. A match is won by using a prescribed set of throws and holds to force an opponent out of a circle approximately fifteen feet in diameter, or by making him touch the ground in or out of the circle with any part of his body. Wrestlers, the champions among whom average over 300 pounds in weight, wear only a thick band of cloth wound around the waist, under the groin, and up the back, and one grips an opponent by this. The use of closed fists, kicking, pulling the hair, and touching below the belt are not condoned. Matches are stunning but brief. Most are over within seconds of the charge: two huge bodies meet in a clash in the center of the ring in a singular show of energy and concentration, and slap and push each other about until in less than a single minute—and usually within the space of about ten seconds—the fight is over. Sumo is extremely simple and to the point.

Sumo, however, is much more than a sport alone. It is a ritual of timeless dignity and classical form. It is a glimpse of ages past, of the history of Japan. Repeated interaction with Shinto religious belief and practice from the early centuries of the Christian era left a profound and indelible mark on the sport. Traces of this heritage can be seen everywhere: in the trappings of the ring, in the pure white twisted rope of cotton (the *yokozuna*) worn by the great champions, and in the smallest and most subtle gestures performed by the wrestlers as they prepare to fight.

There can be no better illustration of sumo's ties with Shinto than the *dohyo matsuri*, or ring ceremony, which takes place inside the wrestling hall on the morning of the day prior to the opening of a tournament. For this three white-robed referees perform the hoary ritual, which is meant to consecrate the wrestling ring and invoke the intervention of the gods to protect the wrestlers from injury during the coming matches, before a formal assemblage of referees, judges, and retired wrestlers, all officials of the organization that controls professional sumo. Kneeling in front of seven wands bearing zigzag strips of folded white paper (*gohei*), which symbolize the gods of creation and of the four seasons, the chief referee lifts his voice in the manner of a Shinto priest: "*Tencho chikyu fu-u junji* (Everlasting life to heaven, long life to earth, and may the winds and rains be seasonable)." A wand is then placed in each of the corners of the wrestling platform, good-luck symbols—torreya nuts, dried chestnuts, kelp, and cuttlefish—are blessed and buried in the center of the ring in an unglazed earthenware pot, and an offering of salt and sakè is made. The austere ritual is concluded as two groups of attendants dressed in happi coats enter the hall, carrying large lacquered drums suspended from poles, and march three times around the ring. One of the drums is later set up on a platform at the top of a bamboo scaffolding, over fifty feet in height, just outside the wrestling hall, and will be beaten to announce the close of each day of wrestling. Then the attendants head into the streets toward predetermined territories to call on stores, restaurants, and each of the sumo training stables to beat the drums and announce the schedule of matches of the highest-ranked wrestlers the following day. This custom is over two hundred and fifty years old: during the Edo period (1603–1868), when there were no permanent, indoor wrestling grounds, tournaments would often be postponed or halted in the middle because of inclement weather. Attendants carrying *fure daiko*, or announcement drums, were therefore always sent out to the entertainment and merchant quarters of the city if matches were to be held the following day. The daily parades of the attendants became unnecessary after the construction of the first permanent wrestling hall in Tokyo in 1909, and today they are used only on the day before the opening of a tournament.

The present form of sumo is of relatively recent evolution, for most of the ceremonial traditions as performed today—including the ring ceremony—date back to no earlier than the late seventeenth century, although a ritualized form of sumo has existed for well over a thousand years. Sumo has endured periodic changes in rules, dress, and even in name as it has adapted to the storms of political upsets and cultural vicissitudes since its origin as a prehistoric Shinto divination ritual. The early grappling form was known as *chikara kurabe*, or strength-testing, while in the beginning of the feudal ages sumo, then called *sumai*, was developed as a martial skill aimed at forcing an enemy to the ground so that he could be taken captive or decapitated. During the Edo period sumo was held as benefit-wrestling contests to raise funds to rebuild shrines and temples, or as street-corner fights between unemployed samurai who wrestled for the coins that spectators would toss into a makeshift ring.

Eventually elements both secular and religious were pulled together to become *ozumo*, or grand sumo, as it is known today. It is the constant interplay of a heritage intrinsically both sacred and profane—the observance of ritual added to the incredible spectacle of three-hundred-pound giants slamming into each other—that makes this indigenous wrestling form the national sport of Japan.

History, Rites, Traditions

1. Origins

Asian Influences Sumo, like many other aspects of Japanese culture, has its origins in the traditions of the Asian mainland. The Japanese islands lie in an arc off the northeast Asian continent, close to the mainland at both the far north and the southwest. While the Ainu tribes, found today only in small numbers on the northern island of Hokkaido and the island of Sakhalin, seem to have been Caucasoid in origin and apparently reached Japan by way of the Kurils or eastern Siberia, the Japanese are basically a Mongoloid race with traces of southern Chinese and Indonesian bloodlines.

Early Japanese wrestling may easily have included elements of Mongolian or Korean ancestry. Japan had cultural ties with Korea from ancient times; Korean influence was especially strong from the sixth to the eighth century, as can be attested to by the excavation of the stone-slab tomb at Takamatsuzuka in Nara Prefecture. The walls of this early-eighth-century tomb are decorated with frescoes reminiscent of paintings found in the T'ung-kou basin of the Yalu River in northern Korea, near the ancient capital of Koguryo, which was the first and largest of the early native states to develop in Korea when the Chinese Han-dynasty colonies there began to decline in the first century B.C. It was populated mainly by Tungusic tribes that had migrated southward from central

Manchuria into the mountains in the far north of Korea. By the fifth century A.D., Koguryo had spread to encompass fully two-thirds of the Korean peninsula and part of Manchuria.

Many of the tombs in the T'ung-kou region contain vivid frescoes of figures, one of the few surviving remnants of the customs of the early Korean noble classes. Among these is the sixth-century "Tomb of the Wrestlers," in which scenes of wrestlers performing to entertain noble guests decorate two of the walls. The figures wear only loincloths. On one wall the wrestlers extend their arms as they leap toward each other to fight; on the other they are posed in a grappling position as an officiating figure looks on. Both are Mongolian-type techniques of wrestling, and both are strikingly similar to early descriptions of sumo.

While any Korean influence on sumo can only be speculated on, that from China can be more readily ascertained from old descriptions of Chinese wrestling in historical documents. Records of wrestling in China date back to the Chou dynasty (1030–221 B.C.). Until around the tenth century A.D., wrestling was commonly known as *chiao-ti* or *chiao-li* and was written with characters meaning horned strength. Chiao-ti originally referred to a rough sort of ritual contest at rural festivities in which men wearing horned caps butted each other, similar to a dancelike game, called *ch'ih yu-hsi*, that was common in Han times (202 B.C.–A.D. 220). By then sophisticated holds and throws had replaced the butting techniques used in chiao-ti, and wrestling had came to be practiced, along with archery and chariot driving, as part of the official military training of the imperial guards.

What was at first a purely military training soon became a favored court amusement. According to the *Shih Chi* (Book of History, first century B.C.), the second Ch'in emperor often amused himself by holding chiao-ti tournaments and musical shows in his palace at Kan Chuan. The founder of the Han dynasty, Liu Pang, attempted to bring a halt to the vulgar displays, but his successor, Han Wu Ti, loved such amusements and revived the shows, turning them into gorgeous spectacles complete with dancers, musicians, and matches between young boys. Chiao-li was added to the official list of court amusements by Ts'ao Ts'ao, the last of the Han rulers, and by the sixth century these matches had become monthly events at the court.

Chiao-li was a major amusement among the commoners as well. Wrestling continued to be performed for rural festivals, and tournaments began to gain popularity in the capital. The *Han Shu* (History of the Han Dynasty, first century A.D.) reported a tournament at the capital, held in the spring of 107 B.C., in which "chiao-ti was

3. *Scene of loincloth-clad wrestlers in a wall painting from the Tomb of the Wrestlers in the T'ung-kou region of North Korea. One of two paintings of wrestlers in the tomb.*

角觝之圖

4. *Ming-dynasty illustration of chiao-ti as it was done in China during the Han period.*

performed, and all those within a radius of 300 miles came to watch."[1] It went on to state that "in the summer of 104 B.C. the people of the capital watched chiao-ti performed at the P'ing Lo Hall at Shang Ming." The poet Chang Heng saw this performance and was moved to write: "I gaze at the mighty arena, and ponder on the marvelous performance of chiao-ti."

By the Sui dynasty (590–618), chiao-ti had become fixed on the lunar calendar for the fifteenth day of the first month (the last day of the New Year's festivities), but this was such an elaborate affair that a memorial was presented to the emperor Yang Ti petitioning him to put an end to this extravagant practice. Yang Ti, however, was himself so fond of the sport that he would go in disguise to see popular wrestling matches in the capital. Wrestling tournaments were also performed on the fifteenth day of the seventh month, both at popular festivals and at the court. During the T'ang dynasty (618–906) emperors held lavish banquets at which chiao-ti, music, and dancing were performed as entertainment. A history of the T'ang period reported that "after the various shows and performances, the officers of the left and right guards would beat on big drums, and those naked strong men would file in and compete in strength to decide who was the winner." From the early T'ang period, wrestling was also called *hsiang-pu,* or mutual beating. During the Sung dynasty (960–1279) it became known as *p'ai-chang,* and later as *shuai-chiao.* The last is the term used for contemporary Chinese wrestling techniques.

As early as the Han dynasty, large numbers of professional wrestlers began to participate in the popular wrestling contests, and especially strong wrestlers were selected to appear at the court festivities, after which they were often made a part of the imperial retinue. Professional chiao-li wrestlers among the soldiers of the T'ang-dynasty armies performed both in the capital and in the provinces. The names and exploits of famous wrestlers were recorded in the national chronicles and poetry anthologies. The *T'ang Yü Lin,* a history of the T'ang dynasty, records: "When Li Hsiang was the military governor of Ta Liang Province, he heard that the coastal guards of the army had brought in four strong fellows by the names of Fu Ch'ang-leng, Shen Wan-shih, Fung Wu-ch'ien, and Ch'ien Tsu-t'ao, all of whom were skilled at boxing and wrestling. He decided to hold a feast for them the following day on the football grounds. For it he had roasted the tendons of cows so old that they were like the chopped-up meat of an elephant callus, and then he had the wrestlers seated on the grass with huge trays of the food. Wan-shih and two of the others saw that the roast was tough and did not dare to eat it. Wu-ch'ien alone closed his eyes tight, opened his mouth, and, picking up the roast with both hands, bit the meat like a tiger. The governor Hsiang saw this and remarked: 'Truly you are the strong one.' He bade the four men wrestle, and Wu-ch'ien alone won."

The emperors of the Sung dynasty, like their predecessors, continued the traditions of wrestling matches held between men chosen from the imperial guards. Some one hundred and twenty wrestlers were kept in the inner gardens of the palace, ready in case the emperor wished to watch them perform. They also wrestled for the important festivals of the court and were ranked according to their performances. Prizes of gold, silver, brocades, and other fine cloths were often awarded. The poet Yang Wan-li wrote "A Poem on Chiao-ti" to describe his feeling after watching one of the imperial matches.

> This marvelous show in the arena, with men matching
>   their talents—
> All this obtains a smile from the heavenly countenance.
> When the chiao-ti is over, the party is over—
> They file out of the palace and return, holding flowers.

The early court-sumo rituals in the Japanese capital were probably affected as early as the eighth century A.D. by the precedents set by the Chinese wrestling tournaments. The influence of Chinese culture had trickled into Japan for centuries by way of Korea, but with the adoption of the Chinese writing system in the fifth century and of Buddhism a century later, cultural adoption and imitation began to accelerate. Direct communication was opened up with the Sui empire in the early seventh century, and envoys and scholars sent to China brought back both books and firsthand knowledge of the ceremonies of the Chinese court. The reading of the classical Chinese anthologies and histories and the observance of Chinese ritual and etiquette became the major concerns of the Japanese court.

Early Records Although sumo drew some of its roots from the Asian mainland, at no point did it relinquish its native flavor. In the former Yamato region, excavations of ancient tumuli have unearthed *haniwa* (clay figures) of wrestlers and Korean-style earthen ceremonial vessels decorated with figurines of wrestlers. These are significant evidence that sumo was preformed as part of Shinto ritual at least from the Tumulus period (250–552).

Shinto, or the way of the gods, is a loosely bound set of shamanistic beliefs rather than an organized or homogeneous religion. In essence it is nature worship, concerned mainly with ritual purity and rites of fertility and divination related to the growth and harvest of crops. The term *kami*, usually translated into English as god or deity, literally means something superior and is used for both animate and inanimate objects. Huge trees, interestingly shaped rocks, rice seedlings, the wind, mountains, and persons of great power can all be kami. Departed ancestors, also known as kami, are honored. Ancestor worship assumed greater importance under the influence of Chinese Confucianist doctrine, while the dominance of the Yamato state resulted in the ideological supremacy of the Yamato-clan deity, the sun goddess Amaterasu.

Despite the existence of early art works depicting wrestling, written records of sumo did not appear until later. Tales concerning sumo were chronicled in the early-eighth-century historical documents of the imperial court, then located in Nara. One of these, found in the *Kojiki* (Record of Ancient Matters, 712), a work that dealt largely with the mythology of the ruling Yamato clan, describes the wrestling match between Takemikazuchi no Kami, a deity, and Takeminakata no Kami, the son of the ruler of Izumo on the Japan Sea coast. The results of this match were said to have established the supremacy of the "divine" Yamato race. The Izumo dynasty was taken over by the Yamato dynasty around the fourth century, but the actual power of the imperial clan was still tenuous enough at the time of the compilation of the *Kojiki* to justify careful handling of the records so as to indisputably establish the Yamato dynasty's legitimacy. The choice of using wrestling as the vehicle for an event no less vital to their position than the inheritance of the nation confirms that in early Japan wrestling was commonly viewed as a means of determining the will of the gods.

Records of early wrestling also appear in the *Nihongi* (The Chronicles of Japan, 720). The early Japanese word for wrestling, chikara kurabe, was written in the *Nihongi* with the Chinese characters used for chiao-li, chiao-ti, and hsiang-pu, depending upon where it appeared. There is no doubt that the records of the elaborate imperial wrestling tournaments on the mainland had already been read by Japanese scholars and noble literati before this account was written. In the *Nihongi*, too, wrestling and sumo were tied to Shinto and the early Japanese deities. The early court tradition of holding ritual-sumo performances on the seventh day of the seventh month was explained in the *Nihongi* in a legend describing how two champion wrestlers, Nomi no Sukune from Izumo

5. *Wooden figurines, called the Engishiki dolls, of sumo wrestlers. The figurines are over one thousand years old.*

and Taima no Kehaya from Yamato, were summoned to the Yamato court to appear before the mythical emperor Suinin on that day in the seventh year of his reign (23 B.C.?).

According to this account, Sukune broke the ribs and loins of Kehaya with a violent kick, killing him, and the land of Kehaya was seized and given to Sukune, who remained in Yamato to serve the emperor. Shrines honoring both Sukune and Kehaya can still be found scattered throughout western Japan. No further mention of Kehaya is made in the early histories, although Sukune is cited elsewhere in the *Nihongi* as the founder of the Hajibe clan of Izumo. This clan was known for producing the ritual implements used at the court and buried in royal tomb sites. According to legend, it was at Sukune's suggestion that figurines were substituted for living attendants at the tombs of imperial family members.

Sumo was mentioned in a number of early court documents as being associated with the seventh day of the seventh month, the date set aside for the annual court sumo tournaments of the eighth and early ninth centuries. According to Chinese legend—at least to one of the many myths ascribed to that day—this was the night when the two star-lovers, Kengyu (the Altair star in Aquila) and Shokujo (the Vega star in Lyra), who were once mortal but had

6. *Scroll painting of Nomi no Sukune defeating the boastful Taima no Kehaya in a wrestling match before the emperor Suinin.*

been banished to the heavens by a jealous deity, crossed the sky on a bridge built of magpie wings for a once-yearly tryst. The concept of the festival, known as Tanabata in Japan, was introduced from the mainland around the middle of the eighth century and became a regular court festivity sometime during the ninth century.

It seems that before then the seventh day of the seventh month was already part of an entirely different festival of a purely agricultural origin. In more recent folk traditions, the date, which coincided with the first quarter of the new moon, was set aside for the cleaning of the graves in preparation for the festival of the dead—Urabon'e or, more commonly, Obon—eight days later. It was a day for purifying the body, and ritual bathing was common practice. A curious old adage cautions against bathing in the river on Tanabata, and translates: "Take care, or you'll be challenged to sumo by the *kappa* [the spirits of the water] and be pulled in!"

The calendar of the festivities of the imperial court was at least partly derived from the native agricultural festivals. Buddhism was officially adopted by the Yamato court in 552, but by the late seventh century the political influence of the Buddhist clergy had grown so great that the court attempted to reverse the trend by reviving the observance of Shinto ritual. Indigenous Shinto practice mixed with Chinese protocol began to color all official ceremony, and traditional rites were revived or newly adopted, while the major imperial shrines rapidly grew in importance. It was around this time that sumo seems to have been adopted by the imperial court as an annual ritual. Significantly, the sumo ceremonies of the Nara and the Heian courts, like the archery contests of the New Year's festivities of the first month and the equestrian archery of the fifth month, were known as *sechie*, an archaic word meaning a festive meal in honor of the deities.

In 734 the Nara aristocracy began officially to imitate the Sui-dynasty wrestling festivals with their own large-scale performances, known as *sumai no sechi*, or court sumo ceremonies, and any traces of the original religious intention behind the performances were discarded as the court conscientiously followed the examples of the Chinese.

Until the early ninth century the court sumo ceremonies were held annually on the seventh day of the seventh month. As the Tanabata festival was adopted by the court to be observed on the seventh day, an imperial edict in the year 824 moved the wrestling performance to the sixteenth day of the month. It was later shifted briefly to the eighth day, and still later to the fifteenth day. The ceremonial codes of the early tenth century finally specified that sumo be held annually on the twenty-fifth and twenty-sixth days of the seventh month, where it remained through the late twelfth century. Shinto ritual observances rapidly lost their religious aura as the tournaments began to imitate the elaborate customs of Chinese wrestling ceremonies, and sumo took its first major step toward becoming the fascinating spectacle it is today.

Rural Traditions and Rituals   No real documentation of traditional Japanese folk practices was made until the early twentieth century, when it suddenly became apparent that the village culture was on the verge of being annihilated under the onslaught of westernization. Residual village festive traditions and studies made by folklorists in the early part of this century give support to theories, based on archeological evidence and the early legends recorded in the eighth-century historical documents, that sumo was practiced as a part of Shinto fertility and divination rituals dedicated to the native spirits.[2]

Sumo performed as a religious ritual during festivals is known as *shinji-zumo,* or god-service sumo. The ancient festivals were almost invariably based on the agricultural calendar and thus linked to the production of rice. *Matsuri,* the word for festival, actually means to serve or entertain superior beings—in this case, the deities. It was only natural that the villages should call upon the guardian spirits during the festivals to assure protection for the maturing crops. Sumo and the other ritual competitions—horse racing (*keiba*), tug-of-war (*tsuna-biki*), and kite flying (*tako age*), all of which were traditionally a part of festivals—were considered as kinds of godly entertainments or divination rituals performed to gain the blessings of the spirits for the coming harvest.

Today a number of these traditional god-service rituals are still practiced. For a wrestling festival held at the Hakui Shrine in Ishikawa Prefecture every year in late September, wrestlers from the nearby districts of Kaga and Etchu are called "those from above the mountain," and wrestlers from the Noto and Sado districts are labeled "those from below the mountain." The wrestling matches are held between these two groups, and the region that is victorious is supposed to be assured of the most successful harvest. On October 24 there is a similar wrestling festival at the Mikami Somoku Shrine in Shiga Prefecture, held as a part of the harvest-thanksgiving festivities. The term *somoku,* which in this case is used as part of the shrine's name, is here written with the characters used for *sumo,* but it is a word that is generally associated with rice crops. Both of these festivals probably originated long ago as divination rituals, when representatives of different villages or clan groups competed for the blessings of the deities.

Other types of sumo also seem to have their origins in a ritualistic rather than in a competitive purpose. The choosing of *toya*, or local shrine officials with one-year terms of responsibility for the Shinto services at the village tutelary shrine, is often conducted by means of sumo. Winning these is indicative of the approval of the deities, and in that sense the matches are quite close in character to the divination festivals. Very often, however, *toya-zumo* is more a highly ritualized dance form than it is a wrestling match. For the final ritual of a festival held in October at the Kasuga Shrine in Kyoto's Kamo district, the two toya for the coming year perform sumo in the presence of the incumbent toya, bleached cotton cloth being wrapped around the wrestlers' otherwise naked bodies. It is not a trial of strength but rather only a ritual in which they join hands and shake them up and down. After repeating this procedure four times, each time alternating positions, the two are presented with halberds decorated with folded strips of white ceremonial paper, and the ritual is concluded. Another toya-zumo is found at the Tenno Shrine in the Yanaka district of Kyoto, performed as part of the Chrysanthemum Festival on September 9.

Another widely practiced custom is the so-called *konaki-zumo*, or child-crying sumo. Children's wrestling was included in the shrine rituals and wrestling tournaments of the Heian court and is still found all over the country. But it seems that child-crying sumo is of quite different origins. In keeping with the old Japanese proverb "a crying child will thrive [*naku ko wa sodatsu*]," this sumo is a staring contest between infants in which the first child to cry is declared the winner and is thus assured of good fortune. Sometimes a tiny loincloth is fastened around the infant, as at the Ujigami Kitare Shrine in Takeda Harbor in Oita Prefecture. At the Kunitsu Shrine in the Kasagi district of Kyoto, infants are held by the toya, and the one to cry first is the loser. Child-crying sumo is usually held in the winter months, after the thankgiving rites for the harvest are over. Sometimes a ring is constructed in front of the shrine, and children born during the previous year are held in this and manipulated in the gestures of sumo.

Tradition at the Momiyama Shrine at Kanuma City in Tochigi Prefecture has it that during the warring years of the feudal period the samurai father of a child who had died shortly after birth went to the shrine to make supplications to the deities. Miraculously, after two full days of prayer, the boy began to breathe once more. It is said that afterwards the shrine came to be known as the Ikiko

(Living Child) Shrine. The festivities there occur on the ninth day of the ninth month by the old calendar, a date that generally falls in November. A ring is constructed in front of the shrine, and young boys of less than one year of age are sat down to watch a puppet show using sumo dolls. The first infant to cry is declared the winner.

In other areas of the country sumo puppet performances are held. At the Koyonomiya and Kohyo shrines in the complex of the Jisa Hachiman Shrine of Nakatsu City in Oita Prefecture, wrestling puppets form part of the rituals of the Hojoe Buddhist memorial services in late October.

Of all the god-service rites presently performed at shrines and temples around the country, the *karasu-zumo,* or crow sumo, of the Kamo Shrine in Kyoto is perhaps the most famous.[3] This ritual, noted for its retention of long-standing traditions, is also known as the *choyo shinji,* as it has from ancient times taken place on the day of the Choyo Matsuri (Double-Sun or Chrysanthemum Festival) in September. The rite is deliberately fashioned to mimic the actions of the *karasu,* or crow, and no doubt specifically concerns the legendary *yata-garasu,* a magical bird of Chinese mythology that was said to have three legs and inhabit the sun. The exact origin of the ritual is obscure. The Kamo Shrine itself is dedicated to the deity Takemikazuchi, who is one of the tutelary deities of the Kyoto region and was said to have been sent down to Izumo by the sun goddess to secure the lands of Japan for her descendants—a task he accomplished by wrestling with the son of Okuninushi, Izumo's ruler.

The festivities of the Kamo Shrine begin on the evening of September 8, when young boys selected to participate in *kodomo-zumo,* or children's sumo, scheduled to follow the "ceremony of the cawing of the crows," are gathered at the shrine for practice matches. The antics of the children draw the majority of the spectators to the festival. However, this tradition probably dates back to not much earlier than the late Edo period, when children's sumo was performed at Edo Castle for the shogun Ienari. The custom caught on immediately throughout the country, and children began to appear as a kind of entertainment in ritual-sumo events held at local shrine festivals. It may have been around that time that children's sumo was added to the autumn festival of the Kamo Shrine. If such is the case, then the crow sumo that precedes the matches of children's sumo, although less widely acclaimed than the latter, should be considered the focal point of the occasion.

The crow sumo follows the general pattern of purely ritual sumo in its clear division between the side of the deity and the side of the secular official. The ceremony takes place in a courtyard to the south of the shrine building. A shrine priest and a secular official are positioned on the corridor that runs along the front of the building so that they are seated to the right and the left at the top of the stairs leading up to the shrine. Two large circles are traced in the dust in front of the building by other officials, who then walk around the rings until they reach the point where they intersect. Facing the shrine, each in turn reads aloud a list of the names of the boys to compete later and then mounts the stairs to place the list before the seated officials. Two more officials, known as *tonedai* (a rank found in particular at important shrines such as Kamo and Ise), approach the courtyard from the south, carrying round mats made of rice straw. They squat down on the ground at the far edge of one of the circles, turn from side to side, and then, in three series of three jumps each, hop like crows toward high conical mounds of sand built up in the center of each circle. Placing the mats in front of these, they then hop back to where they began. Twice more they repeat this procedure, carrying first a bow and arrow and then a short ceremonial sword and a fan and leaning these items against the mounds of sand. On the last trip they sit down on the straw mats, facing each other. Bowing once, each takes up a fan and opens it. Then, in turns, they perform the ritual of the "mimicking of the cry of the crow [*karasu naki no gi*]." The official on the left (from the perspective of the officials seated on the balcony), who is the representative of the shrine priest, cries out *"kaa—"*; the official on the right, the representative of the secular authority, answers with *"koo—."* After repeating this ritual three times, they gather together the mats, bows, arrows, swords, and fans and hop back in a series of three jumps to the point from which they began, where they bow and then retire.

Next, referees dressed in ceremonial garb come forth and lead around the piles of sand the young boys selected to perform in the sumo matches. The referee representing the shrine priest is followed by the young wrestlers, and they circle clockwise three times around the mound on the left and then sit down at its south, facing the building. The referee of the secular side then leads his groups of boys three times counter-clockwise around the mound on the right, after which they also sit down. Then ten sumo matches are performed by the children, thus concluding the ceremony.

A notable aspect of the ritual is the circling procedure executed by the shrine representative as the male crow and the secular official as the female crow. This encircling of the pillars is remarkably similar to the circling ritual attributed to the god Izanagi and the god-

7. *Children's sumo, following the crow sumo at the Kamo Shrine in Kyoto.*

dess Izanami in the early chapters of the *Kojiki*.[4] In this creation myth, Izanagi circles the "heavenly pillar" from the left, and Izanami from the right, upon which they meet, exclaim in wonder, and proceed to give birth to the Japanese islands. Phallic symbolism has always been an important part of Japanese culture. It was common belief that the deities could be summoned down to pillars or the tops of trees, while walking around a pillar seems to have been an ancient ceremony in preparation for conjugal intercourse. Many rituals of god-service sumo are associated with circling movements to the left and the right, and it is possible that ritual sumo originally was related to early fertility ceremonies.

At the Oyamazumi Shrine on the island of Omishima, located in the Inland Sea off the northwest coast of Shikoku, there is a variation of ritual sumo known as *hitori-zumo*, or one-man sumo.[5] The Oyamazumi Shrine unifies a number of branch shrines on Shikoku, although it is itself located on one of the outlying islands. The shrine's sumo ritual, which occurs on the fifth day of the fifth month and the ninth day of the ninth month, is associated with the rice-planting festival. The festival consists of two parts: a rice-planting ritual and the one-man sumo. Documents dating from 1364 mention those ceremonies, indicating the antiquity of the tradition. However, Oyamazumi Shrine was patronized by both aristocrats and warriors from ancient times, and it is likely that the rites that the shrine preserves existed long before those fourteenth-century records would indicate.

One-man sumo takes place on a ring built in front of the shrine's sacred field, which is also where the rice-planting ceremonies are held. The sumo is meant to symbolize a match with the spirit of the rice plant, and it is a foregone conclusion that the human will lose to the spirit. The wrestler, who is chosen from the shrine constituency, first stamps his feet on the ground, rinses his mouth with water, and scatters salt in the ring (all purification rituals used in professional sumo since the late seventeenth century) before crouching into position. He then stands upright and moves three times around the ring to the left, straining as if pushing against an invisible opponent. At length his legs are "seized" by the deity, and he is knocked down to the ground. This is followed by two more matches. In the second one, the man grapples, attacks, and wins, but in the end, after all, the human is thrown down and loses to the spirit.

Today, one-man sumo is also performed at the Sumida Hachiman Shrine of Hashimoto City in Wakayama Prefecture. One-man sumo was so well known during the Edo period that it was parodied by beggars in the entertainment districts and near the professional wrestling grounds of the capital. Oyamazumi Shrine is dedicated to the spirit of the mountains, and it is interesting to note that in a village in Kishu, tradition has it that when a man loses a tool in the mountains it will be recovered quickly if he wrestles with the spirit of the mountains. In this case there is no real differentiation between winner and loser, for the spirits of the mountain are said to be fond of sumo, and one gains their favor simply by grappling with them.

A fondness for sumo is also one of the characteristics attributed to kappa. Today the kappa has been transformed into a mischievous, misshapen imp with a liquid-filled hollow on top of his head, but originally he was the spirit of the water and messenger of the water deities. The kappa is said to challenge to wrestling those who defile the river; during the ensuing match he then pulls his opponents down into the depths of the water. Tales such as these may well have stemmed from rituals in which men actually did "wrestle" with the spirits of the mountains and rivers in a manner similar to that seen today in the one-man sumo at Oyamazumi Shrine.

Like crow wrestling at Kamo Shrine, one-man sumo is not so much a contest of strength as it is an appeasement of some kind, a ritual act of contact between man and spirit. One might link it to *dengaku,* the rice-planting dance. The accessories used in crow sumo are strikingly similar to those used during performances of *kagura,* or ritual Shinto dance. Sumo was pronounced *sumai* until around the tenth century and was, in fact, often written with the character *mai,* meaning dance, instead of the character meaning to beat, which is used in hsiang-pu, the then-current Chinese word for wrestling. Sumai may have originated as a contraction of *su no mai,* or uncostumed dance, designating an indigenous form of dance that contrasts with those of Chinese origin, for which masks and costumes were worn.

God-service sumo and the mainstream of nonreligious wrestling, from which professional sumo was to emerge in the eighteenth century, developed as basically separate traditions from the early eighth century, if not before. The distinction between the two was at no time absolute, however. The annual sumo ceremonies of the Heian court originated from a Shinto divination ritual, and in the ensuing centuries the elaborate etiquette of the court tournaments in turn influenced the forms of sumo in village religious rituals. During the late twelfth and early thirteenth centuries sumo tournaments between warriors were held before the military lords of the time as part of the religious festivities of shrines in Kamakura, the military capital at that time. Sumo became a martial skill during the feudal ages, but by the sixteenth century masterless samurai warriors wandered through the countryside in regions where warfare had subsided. Here they were able to earn a tenuous living by performing sumo at local festivals. Professional wrestling groups developed in the castle towns and major urban centers during the late sixteenth and early seventeenth centuries. In the 1680s the central authorities in Edo restricted the location of public wrestling performances to the precincts of temples and shrines. During the ensuing century professional sumo, under the name *kanjin-zumo,* or religious-benefit sumo contests, formally adopted the many Shinto rituals—some of them from god-service sumo traditions—that came to be inseparable from the modern form of the sport.

2. Popularization

The calabash
and hollyhock flowers
crash against each other;
I wonder which
is going to win?[1]

At the Imperial Court   During the Heian period (794–1185) the Japanese imperial family and court nobility, supported in luxury by great landholdings in the provinces, passed much of the year occupied with ceremonies and rituals. Imperial edicts issued between the seventh and twelfth centuries seemed to deal less with problems of government than with matters of protocol and etiquette, while the power of the court steadily declined. An almost complete control over the emperor was established during the ninth century by the Fujiwara family of nobles, thus making the sovereign little more than a figurehead. In the meantime, the effective authority of the central government over the country was slowly being usurped by powerful provincial clans. Beginning in the early ninth century, members of the imperial family were cut off from the throne and sent out to the provinces, where they spawned two powerful warrior clans, the Minamoto (Genji) and the Taira (Hei-

33

8. *Wrestlers preparing for a tournament-banquet at the imperial court. Heian-period*

ke). By the middle of the tenth century the northern region was racked by family rivalries and civil warfare; crime and disorder were rampant even in the capital itself. Finally in 1185 the military and political control of the country slipped irrevocably into the hands of the warrior clans. To the very end, the emperor and his court spent their days taking part in poetry-writing contests and observing elaborate ceremonial functions.

The practice of holding annual wrestling performances at the court became an established ritual in the early eighth century. In 719 a bureau of champions, in charge of selecting wrestlers to participate in the court tournaments, was established by imperial edict. *Sumai-bito* (wrestlers) were conscripted from the provincial regions as imperial tribute, and proclamations issued to the governors of the outlying provinces ordered them to dispatch to the capital men skilled in horse racing, archery, and sumo. Officials sent on behalf of the left and right garrisons of the imperial guards to recruit strong men skilled in wrestling often went as far as the distant northeastern part of the country, penetrating deep into the mountain areas. In 833 the provinces of Echizen, Kaga, Noto, Sado, Kozuke, Shimo-

scroll by Kose no Kimmochi.

tsuke, Kai, Sagami, Musashi, Kazusa, Shimo-osa, and Awa—
regions stretching from the western tip of Honshu to the most
eastern frontier and including areas of Shikoku and islands off the
northeast coast of Japan—were specifically ordered to supply
wrestlers as annual tribute. These wrestlers were supposed to appear
at the capital a full month prior to the ceremonies: those who were
late were taken into custody, and the governors of the provinces
that had sent them lost their offices.

In 784 the capital was moved north from Nara to Nagaoka, primarily to escape the growing power of the Buddhist clergy. It was
transferred a short distance once more nine years later to a location
that was considered to be more auspicious. The new capital of
Heian (present-day Kyoto) was laid out on the plan of the Chinese
city of Ch'ang-an, with broad streets running in a crisscross pattern
and the imperial residence in a rectangular enclosure in the
northern center of the city. Most of the great court ceremonies,
including sumai, were held in the gardens of the Shishinden, the
main inner-palace building. The wrestling ritual rapidly assumed
large-scale proportions as the aristocracy imitated the splendor of

the Sui and T'ang court ceremonies. In 821 the annual wrestling tournaments were set down in the court ceremonial codes as sumai no sechi, which became one of the three important sechie, or tournament-banquets, the other two being archery on the seventeenth day of the first month and equestrian archery on the fifth day of the fifth month.

Matches were presented between "left" and "right." Wrestlers commissioned by the left office of the imperial bodyguards became the *hidari-gata,* or those of the left, while those chosen by the right office of the guards became the *migi-gata,* or those of the right. All court officials above a certain rank were divided into left and right and assigned to the teams to oversee the preparations for the ceremony. The overall direction of the tournament-banquets was normally undertaken by an imperial prince.

Ten days prior to the tournament an imperial order was sent to the officers of the guards to begin practice matches. The wrestlers were ranked, and two days before the ceremony they were sum-

9. *Large Meiji-era scroll illustrating the tournament-banquet ceremonies of the Heian court. The wrestlers are seen waiting behind curtains on either side of the courtyard. Note the gongs and halberds in front of the musicians for each side, seated in the foreground.*

10. Heian-period wrestlers in loincloths (tosagi). The referee (tachiawase), carrying a bow and a quiver of arrows, sits to the right.

moned to the inner palace to be viewed by the emperor. On the day before the tournament-banquet, the garden of the Shishinden was swept and white sand scattered about the courtyard. Two great drums, two gongs, and thirteen ceremonial halberds were set up on either side of the garden for musicians and dancers, and tents were erected on the east and west sides of the yard for the wrestlers. Screens and bamboo curtains were set out on the corridor along the face of the building for the emperor, imperial family members, high-ranking literati and nobility, and military officials.

The thirty-four wrestlers were the first to enter the garden. They were followed by twelve musicians. Next came the emperor, the crown prince, and aristocrats, all in formal attire. The commanders of the imperial guards approached the emperor and presented him with lists of the wrestlers. Then the referees, or *tachiawase,* sporting quivers on their backs and carrying bows, entered the courtyard, followed by a scorekeeper, or *kazusashi,* also with bow and quiver.

The early tournaments began with three matches between children, known as *warabe-zumo,* but these were later discontinued. The adult wrestlers wore baggy frontal loincloths called *tosagi.* Short swords were tucked into the waistbands of the loincloths, and the wrestlers entered the garden wearing upper robes and black court hats. When they wrestled, everything but the loincloth was removed and placed on a round seat cushion near the southern gate of the garden. To distinguish the wrestlers from each other, those of the left team wore paper hollyhock flowers in their hair, while those of the right team wore calabash blossoms. The artificial flowers of the winner were sometimes given to the next wrestler as a good-luck omen.

A pair of referees, selected from among the imperial soldiers, took turns directing the matches. Two wrestlers approached the area in front of the central stairway of the building and stood facing each other. When the referee raised his hands, the wrestlers marched around glaring at one another, finally contesting when they spotted a favorable opportunity. A winner was determined by throwing or twisting his opponent so as to make him touch the ground. A victory could also be scored by dragging the opponent to one's own waiting area. If a match became too long and drawn out with no decision, both wrestlers were chased out the southern gate, and the tournament proceeded to the next match.

Following each match, the musicians of the winning team beat the drums, struck the gongs, and presented a ritual dance. With each new decision, the scorekeeper made clear the number of winning points for each side by sticking an additional arrow in the ground, the calculation of the number won by each team ultimately determining the victorious side. The champions of the first day were pitted against each other on the second day of the wrestling tournament, followed by informal matches between rankless men or valets of the imperial guards. A short concluding ritual was then performed, first by the left team and then by the right team, after which the tournament-banquet came to a close. Upon withdrawing, the wrestlers were invited to join the guards in celebrations, where they often performed a tug of war to entertain the other guests.

The champion wrestler of each side was known as the *hote* and the next in rank as the *sukete* or *waki*. These rankings were determined prior to the tournament at practice matches (*keiko*) conducted by the officers of the guards. Like the *ozeki* of later times, the champion wrestlers were usually the last to perform. Unruly practices, such as kicking and beating with the fists, were forbidden, and over the years the throwing and twisting techniques grew to be quite sophisticated.

The splendor and frequency of tournament-banquet wrestling performances began to decline from the end of the tenth century as the power and wealth of the imperial court decreased. Sumo's adoption by the imperial soldiers as a military art was reflected in the transfer of the ceremonies from the Shishinden to the Butoku-den, or Hall of Military Virtue, near which were a parade ground and enclosures for equestrian games and archery. Tournament-banquet wrestling was discontinued from 1120 to 1156, when it was temporarily revived under the emperor Goshirakawa. It was performed again in 1174 and one final time in 1185, but by then the sumo tournaments had lost nearly all of the grandeur that marked the early period. Many matches were fixed or ended in draws, and as the court weakened, it became practically impossible to summon wrestlers from the provinces.

In Early Literature   The Heian period produced some of the greatest literary treasures of Japanese history, including that classic of world literature, Murasaki Shikibu's *The Tale of Genji* (Genji monogatari). Many of the works of the time include anecdotes about sumo, and a look at some of these will help to illuminate both the nature and the importance of sumo during the Heian period.

A tale found in the *Gempei seisuiki* (Record of the Rise and Fall of the Minamoto and Taira, mid-thirteenth century) records an account of the succession to the throne on the retirement of emperor Montoku, who reigned 850–58. According to the outcome of a horse race, it had already been decided that the emperor's fourth son, Korehito, would succeed to the throne. The emperor was dissatisfied, however, and proclaimed that it should be redecided by a sumo match between two wrestlers, Ki no Natora and Otomo no Yoshio. Natora, who was chosen to represent Koretaka, the eldest son, was a giant of a man. Yoshio, Korehito's champion, was tiny and weak-looking. The match began, and just when it appeared that Yoshio was about to lose, an enormous water buffalo appeared in response to the prayers of a nearby Buddhist monk. Natora was suddenly divested of all of his strength, and his weaker opponent was able to throw him to the ground. In this manner Korehito is said to have become the emperor Seiwa, who ruled 858–76 and was one of the ancestors of the Minamoto clan.

During the reign of the emperor Reizei (967–69), Tada no Michinaka (another ancestor of the Minamoto clan), Tachibana no Shigenobu, Fujiwara no Chiharu, and the monk Remmo were involved in a conspiracy to raise an army in the eastern provinces against the emperor. One day Michinaka and Shigenobu were practicing sumo in the Nishinomiya palace, and Michinaka was thrown against a latticed window and smashed through it, landing on the ground outside, where other nobles could see him. He was so ashamed and outraged that he pulled out his sword and rushed back inside the building to cut his opponent to pieces. Shigenobu ripped a timber from the balustrade to protect himself, and Michinaka, realizing that he could not win, left the palace in a foul temper. Henceforth the two men were on very unfriendly terms, and Michinaka ended up betraying the conspiracy.

11. *Scene from the* Buge sumo emaki *(Warrior-Sumo Picture Scroll), early Toku-gawa period, by Kano Sansetsu, in which Otomo no Yoshio, aided by the prayers of a Buddhist priest, defeats Ki no Natora, thus securing the emperorship for Korehito.*

In the *Ujishui monogatari* (Tales of the Uji Clan, early thirteenth century) is a story of a scholar who possessed great physical strength. In the midst of preparations for the tournament-banquet one year during the reign of Goichijo (1016–36), a number of wrestlers were assembled in the capital. One day wrestlers from Oshu, in the far north of the country, were walking along the path in front of the Bureau of Learning on the imperial palace grounds and were nearing the south gate when they suddenly bumped into a group of students of the noble class. The nobles, incensed by the incident, refused to let the wrestlers pass. The strong scholar, who was slightly bigger than the others, stepped out and told the wrestlers to turn back. The visiting wrestlers, thinking that it would be unseemly for them, as guests in the capital, to provoke a fight, turned around and retreated. The following day when they approached the same place, they found an even larger group of students waiting for them, with the same large scholar at their head. The wrestler Magami no Narimura of Mutsu, who was the champion of the left team, decided to teach the students a lesson and signaled to one of his companions, a strong and tall wrestler, to kick the large scholar. As he raised his foot, the scholar jumped back, and, catching the wrestler's leg as it swung in the air, he threw him back into the crowd of wrestlers as if he weighed no more than a twig. As the wrestler collapsed to the ground "like a squashed frog," the other wrestlers ran off. The scholar pursued Narimura, who ran for his life toward

40 POPULARIZATION

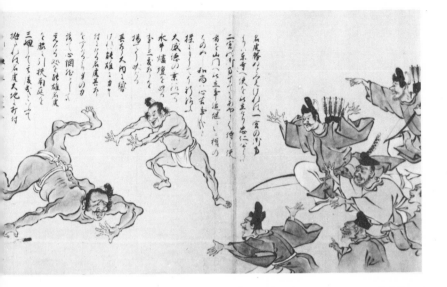

the Sujaku Gate and tried to jump over the wall to the Ministry of Ceremony. As he did so, the scholar grabbed his foot, but Narimura managed to shake off his pursuer and escape over the wall. When he landed, however, he discovered that when the scholar had ripped the sandal from his foot, he had taken the skin of his heel off as well. Later Narimura tried to find out who the young man was, but no one could tell him.

Another story concerning Narimura is set around the same time. The champion wrestler of the right team was Umi no Tsuneyo from Tango Province, just north of the capital, who, while shorter than Narimura, was equally strong. Their match was the last one of the tournament-banquet. As they began to wrestle, Narimura bent over and with all his might shoved his head against Tsuneyo's chest; the latter, however, managed to pull Narimura in and throw him to the ground. Narimura fell, and Tsuneyo collapsed on top of him. For a while neither could get up, for they had fallen with tremendous force. Narimura, who was underneath Tsuneyo, had to be assisted by others because Tsuneyo still had not revived. At length Tsuneyo came to his senses, and Narimura walked over to ask how he felt. "Like an ox!" was the response. As the winner of the tournament, Tsuneyo was given cloth, silver, and gold, all piled in a large mound. He only saw his reward that one time, however, for his ribs had been broken by Narimura, and it is said that he died in Harima Province on his way home.

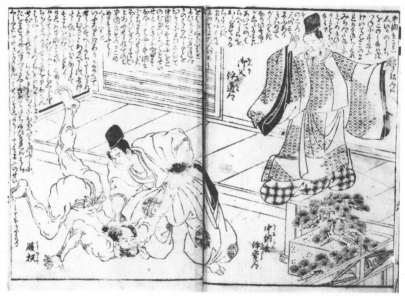

12. *The minister Koremichi watches his son Korezane vanquish Hara-eguri, the Stomach Driller. From the seventeenth-century* Honcho sumo kagami *(Records of Sumo in Japan).*

There is also a story concerning a junior counselor by the name of Korezane, who enjoyed sumo and horse racing so much that he neglected his studies. His father, the minister Koremichi, attempted to persuade him to stop his frivolous pastimes and proposed to him that he challenge the famous wrestler Hara-eguri. If Korezane won, he could do as he wished, but if he lost, he had to give up sumo altogether. Hara-eguri (Stomach Driller) was famed for his technique of digging his head into his opponent's stomach. Korezane agreed to his father's ultimatum. When in the match Hara-eguri ducked his head and began to bore into the junior counselor's stomach, however, Korezane calmly reached over and lifted the wrestler upward by the knots of his loincloth, pulling in such a way that the wrestler's neck came close to breaking. Hara-eguri, unable to stand the pain, collapsed on the ground. Korezane's father was astounded, but had to honor his promise. Hara-eguri, meanwhile, was so ashamed that he ran away.

During the reign of the emperor Toba (1107–23), a wrestler from Owari Province by the name of Koguma no Koreto and his son Korenari paid a visit to the grand counselor Moro no Nagazane.

13. Saiki no Uchinaga, his hand caught by the powerful Takashima no Oiko, is forced to follow her home rather than continue on his way to the sumo tournament in the capital.

At that time there was another wrestler, called Hiromitsu, who was also visiting. The three of them were served wine, and as they got a bit drunk, Hiromitsu began to talk too much and insisted that any wrestler who was big enough could become a champion those days. That touched off an argument, and Korenari and Hiromitsu eventually decided to have it out in a sumo match. They began to wrestle, and Korenari grabbed the hands of his opponent so that the other could not move. Hiromitsu complained that it did not count, so they went out into the garden, stripped off their clothes, and began to wrestle in earnest. Korenari again grabbed Hiromitsu's hands and pulled them down, causing the latter to fall on his face. When Hiromitsu once more insisted on repeating the match, Korenari caught his hands and threw him over so that he landed flat on his back. Weeping in shame, Hiromitsu retired and later became a monk.

A story in the *Kokonchomonshu* (Stories Written and Heard of the Ancient and Modern, 1254) tells of a powerful woman who was adept at wrestling. On the way to the capital for the tournament-banquet, a wrestler from Echizen by the name of Saiki no Uchinaga passed under a stone bridge in the village of Takashima in Omi Province. There he spied a beautiful young woman balancing a pail of water on top of her head. The wrestler succumbed to temptation and reached his hand out to touch the inside of her arm. The woman let out a laugh and pressed her upper arm close to her rib cage, trapping Uchinaga's hand in the pit of her arm. She continued on her way, and the wrestler, unable to pry himself loose, ended up at the woman's hut. There the woman put down her pail and released Uchinaga's hand. When she heard that the wrestler was on his way to the tournament-banquet wrestling, the woman nodded her head a while, thinking, and then remarked: "Isn't that rather dangerous? The capital is huge, and there will no doubt be a great many powerful and magnificent wrestlers. You are not exactly weak, but you are not yet quite the level of a wrestler who might succeed at the capital. Since we just now rubbed each other's sleeves [that is, since we happen to have met by chance like this], there must be a reason. If there is time before the tournament, stay here with me, and I will make you stronger." So Uchinaga stopped for a while and at length became a powerful wrestler. The woman, Takashima no Oiko, owned a great many rice fields and was said to have moved a great stone that would normally have taken a hundred men to budge, in order to fix a broken dike. The stone was still there, said the account, and was called the "dike stone of Oiko."

As the warrior class seized the reins of political power in 1156 and fighting broke out between the Taira and Minamoto clans, tournament-banquet sumo was abolished. While the touramentbanquets were stopped, the sumo tradition continued to thrive. Those wrestlers who had participated in the court tournaments and did not stay in the capital as soldiers returned to their native provinces, spreading familiarity with the refined technique and etiquette of the court sumo to the far reaches of the country. The rise of the warrior class in the late years of the Heian period saw the military adopt sumo as a combat training skill. In the shift of political power from the imperial court to the samurai class, sumo took on a new direction.

As a Military Art In 1156, upon the death of the retired emperor Toba, bitter conflict broke out over the control of the imperial court. The warriors of the powerful Taira and Minamoto clans joined in the fighting. Two violent outbreaks of civil warfare during the ensuing four years left the Minamoto clan defeated and the emperor Goshirakawa on the throne. The real power of government, however, had been transferred to the Taira, and for twenty years the court was dominated by Taira no Kiyomori, who had emerged victorious from the wars of 1156 and 1159 as the head of a mixed group of Taira and Minamoto warriors. In 1180, Minamoto no Yoritomo, the son of a warrior named Yoshitomo who had sided with the Taira in 1156 but was killed as he led an army against them in 1159, gathered together warriors of the Kanto region of eastern Japan and launched a revolt against Kiyomori. While Yoritomo was seizing control of the Kanto Plain, his younger brother, Yoshitsune, captured the capital. The Taira warriors were chased westward along the Inland Sea until they were finally annihilated in 1185. Four years later the whole of Japan was brought under the military control of Yoritomo. Although in theory he was merely a grand general (shogun) acting as the military arm of the emperor in Kyoto, the headquarters he set up in Kamakura in the east became the effective capital of the country. Yoritomo placed his vassals as protectors overseeing the governorships of the provinces and set up loyal retainers as stewards of the vast estates he had confiscated from the court and the opposing clans.

Almost before it had gotten under way, however, Yoritomo's line was actually brought to an end, for he had eliminated his brother for suspected rivalry and left only two weak sons when he himself died in 1199. The Hojo clan, who were relatives of Yoritomo's widow, took control of the government as regents and remained in that position until the final fall of the Kamakura shogunate in 1333. Time itself weakened the personal bonds of loyalty that held the provincial overlords together, while the attempted invasions of Japan by the Mongols in 1274 and 1281 wreaked havoc on the economy of the domains. Local rivalries came to the fore when the emperor Godaigo rebelled against the dominance of Kamakura. The shogunal troops captured the emperor and sent him into exile, but other warrior factions joined in the revolt. When the emperor escaped in 1333, Ashikaga Takauji, who had been sent to capture him, changed loyalties and seized the capital on behalf of Godaigo. At the same time revolts in the eastern regions of the country ended in the capture of Kamakura and the destruction of the Hojo regents. A final insurrection by Godaigo in 1336 ended in failure, and he escaped to set up a second court, which lasted for fifty-four years, south of Nara at Yoshino. Takauji placed another emperor on the throne in Kyoto and assumed the title of shogun in 1338, but the Ashikaga shogunate never acquired the power of the early Kamakura shoguns. Local military clans quickly began to assume control over the provincial domains. The Muromachi period (1336–1568), so named because the Ashikaga shoguns established their headquarters in the Muromachi district of Kyoto, was one of almost incessant warfare during which the Ashikaga shogunate lost all but nominal power over the provinces long before its complete deposition in 1573.

During this period wrestling was primarily considered to be a martial art. Warfare in feudal Japan was conducted as a number of individual encounters between warriors, and on the battlefield, wrestling was an indispensable skill. Sumo was adopted as a basic tenet of the warriors' training, along with swordsmanship, archery, and equestrian arts. As a preparatory exercise for mortal combat, sumo became more complex, and new techniques were devised. Emphasis was laid on throwing the opponent to the ground and pinning him there so that he could be killed or subdued. A direct result of the refinement of warrior sumo was the development of jujutsu, which remained undifferentiated from sumo until the late sixteenth century.

The use of sumo tactics in battle is described in contemporary war tales. The *Gempei seisuiki* contains a detailed narrative of a battle fought at Kotsubo between the warriors Tsuzuri Taro (a vassal of Hatakeyama Shigetada, one of the most famous warriors of the Kamakura period) and Wada Kojiro. Tsuzuri, described as an expert in the techniques of sumo, cast aside his weapons and wrestled with Wada, a retainer of the Miura clan. After a violent match, Wada lost and was decapitated.

Accompanying its diffusion as a martial skill was the inclusion of sumo in the military games of the samurai class. Wrestling matches known as *no-zumo* (field sumo) provided sport for warriors between battles. In 1176, four years before participating in the attacks on the capital that left Yoritomo the military commander of the country, warriors from Izu and Sagami held an impromptu celebration at Kashiwa Pass along the road between Ito and Shuzenji on the Izu Peninsula. Sumo matches formed part of the entertainment, and the champion wrestler, Matano Goro, emerged victorious over twenty-one wrestlers in a row. He then goaded a warrior by the name of Kawazu Saburo into fighting him and was promptly defeated. Matano refused to admit the defeat, insisting that he had lost his footing when he tripped over the root of a tree. Matano seized Kawazu and lifted him high off the ground, but Kawazu beat him with a leg trip—a technique later called a *kawazu-gake* (Kawazu trip). Matano was outraged and humiliated by the incident, and for a while a threat of bloodshed hovered over the

14.   Kawatsu Saburo throwing Matano Goro at Kashiwa Pass. Woodblock-print triptych by Kunisada.

festivities. At length the sulky wrestler was quieted down, but he parted company in a foul temper and arranged to have Kawazu assassinated during his homeward journey. The murder was the catalyst of an eighteen-year-long vendetta waged by two of Kawazu's sons, Soga Juro and Soga Goro, and became the basis for a book known as the *Soga monogatari* (Tales of the Soga Clan).

The feudal lords encouraged the popularization of martial games. Wrestling matches, horse-racing contests, and archery competitions were performed in the precincts of shrines during local festivals and at the mansions of the provincial governors. The *Azuma kagami* (Mirror of the East, c. 1270), which documents the history of the Kamakura shogunate between 1180 and 1256, lists fourteen occasions on which the successive shoguns viewed sumo tournaments during that period. The first was in 1189, when Yoritomo watched sumo matches, mounted archery performances, and horse racing as part of a festival at the Tsurugaoka Hachiman Shrine in Kamakura.

Tales of Warrior-Wrestlers   The champions of sumo and the anecdotes concerning them during the feudal period were invariably linked with the warrior class. Tales of wandering samurai who made circuits of the provinces, boasting of their prowess in wrestling and challenging the local champions before the shogun or provincial daimyo overlords, dot the literature of the period.

One of the most famous warrior-wrestlers of the early Kamakura period was Hatakeyama Shigetada, a vassal of the shogun Yoritomo. At the time there was a warrior by the name of Nagai who was famed as the most powerful wrestler of the eight eastern provinces. Nagai traveled to Kamakura to ask permission from Yoritomo to wrestle with Hatakeyama, and a match was arranged on the spot. Nagai grabbed at Hatakeyama, but Yoritomo's champion held his opponent at arm's length by grasping his shoulders. Not letting Nagai come any closer, he tightened his grip until the other collapsed on the ground. Hatakeyama then quietly resumed his seat near his lord. Nagai's shoulder blades were completely smashed, and he was never again able to wrestle.

One of the most famous wrestlers of the Inland Sea provinces in the early sixteenth century was Wakasugi Saburo, a retainer of the Ouchi clan of Nagato Province. When the head of the clan, Ouchi Yoshioki, went to Kyoto, he took Wakasugi with him. There only one wrestler, a man in the service of the Yamane family, was thought capable of matching Wakasugi, and the Ashikaga shogun Yoshitane ordered the two to wrestle. The Ouchi champion won, but the spectators, who favored the local wrestler, complained that the match had been fixed, causing Wakasugi to fume in rage. Lifting his opponent high above his head, he threw him to the ground with a tremendous yell. The unfortunate wrestler coughed up blood and died immediately.

One day a wrestler by the name of Sorihashi from Chikuzen Province appeared at the castle of Lord Terazawa, governor of Karatsu Province. Terazawa's foot soldiers and younger samurai were no match for him, so the lord asked one of his greatest warriors, Toyama Rokubei, to wrestle with him. The two faced each other in the courtyard. Sorihashi stooped and rushed at his opponent, but the warrior caught hold of the knots of the wrestler's loincloth and lifted him off the ground with one hand. He swung Sorihashi in the air several times before throwing him down with a loud yell. The wrestler lay sprawled on the ground, unconscious. When he finally woke, he found that his left arm had been smashed and the bones dislocated. He remained ever after a cripple.

Chosokabe Motochika (1539–99), the powerful daimyo of Tosa Province, was fond of sumo. He was known to gather wrestlers together for a tournament every year on the evening of the annual

15. *Sumo performed for the shogun Yoritomo at Kamakura in 1189. From a woodblock-print triptych by Kuniyoshi.*

taxation day, which was in the eighth month. The wrestler Genzo of Izumo, while wandering through the provinces performing sumo, heard that Motochika enjoyed wrestling and decided to visit Tosa. No sooner had he arrived than he was summoned to a feast in his honor hosted by the lord, Motochika. After Genzo had retired to his nearby lodgings in Maehama, Motochika and his retainers exchanged looks of surprise at Genzo's size, for he stood almost six and a half feet in height and was so huge that his legs would not fit into an ordinary *hakama* (divided skirt). The daimyo asked his vassals for a volunteer to fight with Genzo, so that at least the powerful wrestler might have an opponent worthy of him. A warrior named Hisaman Hyogo stepped forward to take the challenge. Asked by the lord in what manner he would attempt to handle the visitor, Hyogo replied: "A wrestler of such great power as Genzo would rely heavily on that strength and not pay much attention to subtle technique. When he opens his arms to grab me, I will slip in and take him by his sash. If I can succeed in getting a grip, I cannot fail." The match took place with Motochika and his family in attendance. Hyogo threw the great Genzo with ease as he had planned, and the lord was so pleased that he awarded the young soldier with a sword. Genzo, too, was given five bolts of summer-weight cloth and a mound of coins. The following day a ceremony was held in honor of Hyogo, during which the champion was presented with a citation from Motochika stating that his action was a great honor to the entire province and that, although sumo seemed at times to be a rather foolish activity, it was indeed worthy of being counted among the other martial arts.

The century covering 1467 to 1568 was one of constant warfare between the local feudal overlords. As the warring daimyo gained in power, the Ashikaga shoguns and many of the great families lost their authority and disappeared. In 1568 a lesser daimyo by the name of Oda Nobunaga captured the capital at Kyoto on behalf of the last Ashikaga shogun. During the ensuing fourteen years Nobunaga set about extending his authority over most of Japan, before finally being killed in 1582. Toyotomi Hideyoshi, one of the guardians appointed by Nobunaga for his infant heir, gained the support of Nobunaga's old allies, and by 1590 Hideyoshi had unified all of Japan for the first time in centuries. Neither Nobunaga nor Hideyoshi ventured to assume the old title of shogun after the last Ashikaga ruler was deposed in 1573. Both were content instead to draw authority from the destitute Kyoto emperor as regents to the impotent throne.

Oda Nobunaga's passion for wrestling was notorious. He sponsored a number of huge sumo tournaments between 1570 and 1580 to advertise the vastness of his wealth and power. On one occasion he went so far as to order sumo performed in the imperial palace in Kyoto. The first record of a tournament patronized by Nobunaga says that he viewed sumo while resting at the Joraku-ji temple of Omi Province in 1570. According to the *Nobunaga koki* (Chronicles of Nobunaga): "Nobunaga decided to stay here for a while, and as an entertainment he summoned sumo wrestlers from all over the country to have them perform. All of them were experts, and each took part in the sumo, hoping to be blessed with glory. They displayed with all their might such techniques as *kamo no irikubi* [the stooping neck of the goose], *mizu-guruma* [water wheel], *sori* [bending], *hineri* [twisting], and *nage* [throwing]. Each technique was excellently performed, and Nobunaga was fascinated and enjoyed himself tremendously."[2] Nobunaga organized great sumo tournaments at his castle at Azuchi twice in 1578 and once in 1580. It is reported that at one of the tournaments in 1578 some 1,500 wrestlers were summoned to compete.

Hideyoshi, who was known for his sometimes eccentric behavior, is reported to have summoned together the two greatest wrestlers of the time, Irie Okuranosuke and Toku Inosuke, to perform sumo.

16. *Woodblock print showing sumo performed before Hideyoshi. Kato Kiyomasa, a famous general, is seated in the middle of the right panel, while Hideyoshi is the smaller figure seated in the upper left of that panel.*

The two bowed once to each other and locked firmly together, "not unlike the sculptures of the two Buddhist guardian kings." Hideyoshi stopped the match before a winner was decided, content merely to have been given an exhibition of their strength. It was reported that the other daimyo in attendance were deeply impressed by their lord's action.

Hideyoshi turned the regency over to his nephew Hidetsugu in 1591, although in his position as adviser he firmly held on to the reins of the government. Hidetsugu was known to have retained over one hundred wrestlers among his vassal warriors. On one occasion he summoned wrestlers from the regions around Kyoto for an impromptu night tournament, where, under the light of thousands of candles, he and his feudal lords sat in attendance. The regent's wrestlers sat on the east side of the makeshift theater, and some 300 guest wrestlers sat on the west.

As Entertainment Military strategy changed drastically over the latter half of the sixteenth century. Portuguese traders reached Japan in 1543 and brought with them advanced Western military

As ENTERTAINMENT 51

technology, and by 1570 musket corps using firearms were being deployed in battle in Japan. The new style of mass warfare contributed to a rapid decline in the use of hand-to-hand combat between individual warriors.

To withstand the onslaught of the new guns and cannon, the wealthier feudal lords built massive castles. Large standing armies congregated at the castle sites, and towns sprang up to accommodate them. Whereas Kyoto had previously been the sole metropolis and center of culture for the entire country, the castle towns—Osaka, Edo, Himeji, Fushimi, Sendai, Nagoya, and others—of the daimyo began to emerge as important urban centers by the late sixteenth century.

As the earlier years of the sixteenth century spawned unemployed swordsmen who wandered the country to test their blades, so did the end of that century see ever-increasing numbers of masterless warrior-wrestlers who were forced to earn a living by traveling from province to province, calling for matches with local champions. As the tournaments sponsored by Oda Nobunaga and Toyotomi Hidetsugu stimulated sumo's emergence as a form of popular entertainment in the prospering new castle towns, great wrestlers of both warrior and non-warrior background performed not only before the provincial lords, but also at shrine festivities in urban centers. The matches that took place in the precincts of shrines and temples before audiences of warriors and peasants came to be known as kanjin sumo, or benefit sumo contests.

Kanjin, a term of Buddhist origin, referred in general to some type of fund-raising campaign for a religious institution. Donations were thought to contribute to one's personal accumulation of spiritual merit. When money was needed for the construction or repair of shrine buildings, bridges, or roads, it was customary to have some kind of entertainment performed for that purpose. Admission fees were collected and then donated to further the cause in question. The term kanjin was affixed to such performances, which included *kanjin sarugaku* (the prototype of Noh drama), *kanjin dengaku* (ritual Shinto dance), and kanjin-zumo. Ritual sumo, like the ritual dengaku-dance forms, had always been performed at shrines, so it was natural that such entertainments were chosen to be held as benefits. By the mid-Muromachi period, benefit-sumo performances were so well established that the shogunate attempted to levy a special tax, known as *sumai sen,* on these matches.

In early benefit sumo, groups of wrestlers, called *kanjin-gata* (kanjin side) or *moto kata* (original side), were organized by a temple or shrine to wrestle with volunteers from the audience. This

17. Benefit sumo at the Kamo Shrine in Kyoto. The arena is screened off by curtains, while the drum on the bamboo scaffolding in the center was used to summon spectators. Detail of an early Edo-period folding screen.

manner of wrestling was popularly known as *tobi iri,* or flying entrance. The ring was delineated by a circle formed by wrestlers and spectators seated on the ground; challengers sprang up from around the ring to wrestle with a defending champion in the center. Often a wrestler would take on a succession of challengers until he was himself replaced by a new champion. A wrestler won by throwing his opponent down to the ground or pushing him out into the audience.

Humorous tales dating from the early seventeenth century include accounts of benefit sumo as it began to develop into large-scale performances in the late sixteenth century. The *Kiyushoran* (Glimpses of Entertaining Things, compiled 1818) relates:

Shortly after the construction of Hideyoshi's Fushimi Castle in Kyoto in 1594, famous sumo wrestlers arrived from the various provinces to participate in benefit sumo at Uchi no Nanahonmatsu. Among the benefit-sumo wrestlers were Tateishi, Fushiishi, Araima, Sorihashi, Kurokume, Oikaze, and others—altogether some thirty wrestlers. The guest wrestlers came not only from the five home provinces surrounding Kyoto but also from remoter regions as well. As might be expected from the organizers of the sumo, the wrestlers of the kanjin side won all of the matches. Some of the guest wrestlers were heard to murmur: "It's a shame, but who can really match them?" as they discussed among themselves who might possibly win.

On the last day of the sumo tournament, the wrestler Tateishi, who was the champion of the host team, came out to wrestle. The referee called out to those assembled: "Is the sumo performance entirely exhausted of talent? If there is anyone who would volunteer, step forward and name yourself." But no one volunteered.

Just then, from the corner near the entrance, a voice called out: "Hold the sumo, here is one who would volunteer." The referee answered: "If that is so, then come out immediately." While the spectators wondered at who the heroic man might be, out stepped a young nun of about twenty years of age.

"What an extraordinary person this is!" exclaimed the referee. The woman responded: "So I am. I come from the Kumano area and have been observing these young men wrestling." Tateishi, the wrestler, snorted: "Such a weakling you are! Why, I could take on ten or twenty of you with no trouble. How can you so brazenly dare to attempt to wrestle with me?" The nun insisted, however, that she would wrestle with the champion Tateishi or with none at all.

Both the noble and the humble of the spectators found the incident increasingly interesting, and all cried out to Tateishi to wrestle with her. The nun removed her robe, revealing pantaloons of the Nagasaki style. The referee signaled the beginning of the match, and Tateishi stood up, spread his arms wide, and took a firm stance. The nun trotted forward and began to push him backwards. The audience was delighted and began to applaud. Tateishi was mortified. He took a crouching position and began to wrestle in earnest, grabbing the left arm of the woman. The nun then grasped his thigh from behind and threw him deftly to the ground.

The spectators burst into uncontrollable laughter. Three more wrestlers challenged the nun, but she threw them all down one by one, using a technique so fast that no one could tell how she did it.

Later, when there was again benefit sumo at Fushimi, the same nun participated. She also appeared at Daigo and in Osaka, and, wherever there were great sumo matches, she would take part in them. The people at large thought her extraordinary and feared her, and rumors spread that she was the rarity of the age.[3]

Hideyoshi died in 1598, leaving only an infant as heir to the Toyotomi line, since Hidetsugu was already dead. The most powerful of the contenders for the leadership of the country was Tokugawa Ieyasu. By 1600 Ieyasu had destroyed a coalition of western feudal lords who had resisted his authority, and three years later he took on the rank of shogun, establishing a line of rulers who would continue to govern the country until 1868.

It was the peculiar development of benefit sumo during the over two and a half centuries of peace under the Tokugawa shoguns that gave to sumo the character that so distinguishes its performance today.

3. Beginnings of
Professional Sumo

In Early Edo   In 1615 Ieyasu, who had been assigned the old title of shogun by the Kyoto court in 1603, razed Osaka Castle and destroyed the last pocket of resistance to his rule. In the same year he rebuilt the palace at Kyoto in a show of support for the emperor, from whom his power was nominally drawn, but whom he actually dominated as firmly as he did his feudal vassals. He built a system of tight control over the daimyo and their private domains, based on the strategic allocation of collateral Tokugawa families and vassals throughout the country. But the overriding theory behind the social and political policies of Tokugawa rule was that of stability by the institutionalization and preservation of the status quo. Ieyasu issued strict codes of regulation to govern the lives of the warrior class. Toyotomi Hideyoshi had decreed a freezing of social status in 1590, forbidding any further mobility between classes and outlawing the carrying of arms by peasants. Ieyasu continued both Hideyoshi's proscription on social mobility and his distinct separation of the classes. As a result, samurai were to be considered far above commoners in status, and contact between the two classes was strictly regulated.

In the late sixteenth century Hideyoshi had set up a hostage system, requiring the wives and children of the daimyo to reside permanently in his capital in order to insure the continued fealty of the provincial lords; in 1635 Ieyasu made this system mandatory. Hostages were sent to the new capital of Edo, where a great castle had been completed in 1606. In addition, most of the daimyo were required to spend every other year in residence in the new military capital. The lords built great mansions and permanently transferred large numbers of their vassals to Edo, where a populace of merchants and servants immediately began to develop to service them. By the late eighteenth century Edo, a mere village two hundred years earlier, had grown to a metropolis with a population of nearly one million.

Along with the continued peace and stability of the country and the constant traveling of the processions of the daimyo over the major highways, there was a growth in commercial activity. Although Edo itself remained heavily dominated by its warrior population for over a century after the founding of Tokugawa rule, in the western urban centers of Osaka and Kyoto a new merchant culture began to emerge by the mid-1600s. Amusement centers flourished in the rapidly growing cities, complete with theaters, restaurants, baths, and houses of prostitution, as a culture developed that was for the first time in Japanese history characterized not by the aesthetic tastes of the elite society of nobles and warriors, but rather by mass participation in the world of entertainment. Repeated efforts were made by the authorities to curb the activities of the amusement districts, largely because of the inevitable clashes that occurred there between the samurai and merchant classes, but the culture of the townsmen continued to prosper. By the latter half of the eighteenth century the center of the new culture moved from Osaka to Edo, which then became not only the political headquarters of the country but also the cultural capital.

The early years of Tokugawa rule were marked by the existence of massive numbers of samurai who had lost their lords through death or deposition during the political upheaval of the previous period. These *ronin,* or masterless samurai, were forbidden by law to join the ranks of the lower classes, but with lasting peace it was difficult to locate new masters among the daimyo lords or *hatamoto* (bannermen). Sumo was one of the few as yet ill-defined occupational niches left in the otherwise rigid hierarchical social structure of the period. The daimyo continued to recruit samurai to wrestle as part of their *geisha-gumi,* or men specializing in the martial arts, and raised them to the status of vassals, complete with stipends. During the early years of the Edo period, the collateral Tokugawa lords of Kishu, the Maeda of Saga, the Ikeda of Tottori,

18. Detail from the scroll painting Tsuji-zumo no zu (Street-corner Sumo Scroll), depicting itinerant wrestlers plying their trade. Late sixteenth or early seventeenth century.

the Matsudaira of Fukui, the Sakai of Himeij, and the Hosokawa of Kumamoto were among those daimyo who retained large numbers of wrestlers included in their warriors.

At the other end of the scale, unemployed warriors often performed in informal *tsuji-zumo,* or street-corner wrestling matches, in the entertainment districts of the castle towns, battling over coins thrown into the ring by spectators. Semiprofessional sumo ronin also gathered together groups of wrestlers and organized benefit-sumo performances at shrines and temples in both the provinces and the developing urban centers.

The earliest extant reference to benefit sumo in Edo is a brief mention in a work dated 1643 and titled the *Azuma monogatari* (Tales of the Eastern Provinces). In a description of the Nihombashi section of Edo, the author stated: "Walking through Temmamachi and arriving at Inugimachi, I heard by chance the singing of ballads and the sounds of the samisen, flutes, biwa, koto, and both large and small drums. When I inquired as to what was happening, those about me replied that it was performances of Kabuki drama by the great Murayama Sakan from Satsuma, the puppet theater, and benefit sumo. A number of other performances could be seen as well. . . ."[1] At that time benefit sumo was common in the gay

quarters, where it existed alongside theatrical performances as an entertainment. It can be supposed that during the previous three decades, when shrines and temples were erected en masse in the new capital city, benefit sumo was held in the entertainment districts to raise money for their construction.

Edo in the early seventeenth century was a rough town. Samurai retained by the overlords, unemployed ronin, and ruffians of the peasant class swaggered side by side through the city streets. It was thus inevitable that sumo in Edo led to bloody quarrels and disputes. Unlike in Kyoto, where orderly benefit-sumo contests on temple grounds were already an established tradition, Edo sumo performances were highly prone to violence. What was particularly alarming to the authorities was the informal street-corner matches that took place in the entertainment districts. Unemployed warriors and rough townsmen came into violent contact in these street-corner contests fought for small amounts of money tossed down by the onlookers who gathered around the impromptu wrestlers. Clashes between hot-tempered masterless samurai and commoners were incessant; drawn swords and the untimely death of a combatant or spectator were not unheard of.

Public disturbances arising from the performance of wrestling matches became serious enough to compel the Edo authorities to take action. In 1648 the town magistrate decreed the following bans, which were posted on wooden planks at street corners throughout the city:

Item: Street-corner sumo shall not be performed.
Item: Benefit sumo shall no longer be organized.
Item: Wrestlers who are invited to perform at the residences of their superiors shall not wear loincloths made of silk, but only those of plain cotton cloth.[2]

Even in the months immediately following the bans against public sumo, however, the Edo authorities officially condoned a six-day-long performance of benefit sumo for the ground-breaking ceremonies of the Sanjusangendo temple in the Asakusa district in the eastern part of the city. After a lengthy debate over the validity of the petition presented by the temple authorities, the city magistrate issued permission for the event, with the conditions that no donations be made for the performance itself and that challengers from the crowd not participate in the matches.

Three years later the discovery of the ill-fated conspiracy of a group of masterless samurai to overthrow the Tokugawa government led to the proclamation of a number of edicts in Edo. One of the bans outlawed the use of *shikona,* or assumed wrestling names. The prohibition was primarily directed not at wrestlers or other practioners of the martial arts, most of whom had customarily assumed professional names from early Muromachi times, but at the knight-errants and vagabonds of the city, who tended to adopt fanciful names. In addition, regulations concerning the activities of the entertainment districts were tightened, and investigative surveys were ordered of all of the masterless samurai in the capital. Official exhortations to the daimyo advised strict economic measures, and such extravagances as private Kabuki performances and exhibitions of sumo were harshly criticized. Because of the censure by the Tokugawa authorities, the practice of hiring wrestlers as a part of the daimyos' entourages stopped almost completely for the next three decades.

The entertainment districts of Edo continued to attract flocks of vagrants and unemployed samurai, and, in spite of the strict bans against performing sumo for money, illicit matches on streets and in shrine precincts permitted samurai to wring a tenuous living out of a wrestling profession. Once again, because of the growing incidence of bloodshed accompanying the abuse of the regulations concerning sumo, proclamations were issued in 1661 banning wrestling contests. The edicts, while specifying that theatrical performances of Noh, Kabuki, and Bunraku were to be restricted to certain defined sectors of the city, totally prohibited sumo of all types within the city limits.

Official Recognition For over two decades sumo floundered in a state of stagnation while the other Edo-period entertainments flourished and gained refinement in the major cities. Fragmentary pictorial and documentary evidence, as well as periodic edicts against sumo, testify, however, to the continued existence of the illicit wrestling matches. In self-defense, professional wrestlers and masterless samurai began to band together in loose coalitions to petition the authorities for permission to perform. Finally in 1684 the masterless samurai Ikazuchi Gondaiyu obtained permission from the shrine magistrate of Edo to hold an eight-day performance of benefit sumo in the precincts of Fukagawa Hachiman Shrine in the eastern part of the city. After a number of unsuccessful attempts, Gondaiyu included in the final, successful petition to the magistrate detailed innovations intended to circumvent the problems of earlier sumo tournaments. One of these was the defining of a wrestling ring by placing bales of earth around the wrestling area.

Until the second half of the seventeenth century there was no fixed wrestling ring. Instead, wrestlers and spectators formed a circle (*hito kataya*) around the wrestling area. The earliest illustration of a definite ring is a painting dating to the 1660s or early 1670s of a sumo match in the Shijo-gawara district of Kyoto, in which four pillars were set up with cords strung between them to form a square area.

The ring (*dohyo*) itself dates from around the late 1660s. The earliest portrayal of a ring appears in a folding-screen painting by the Tosa school done between 1673 and 1681; the term "dohyo" was used to refer to the *sumoba* (the area in which the wrestling occurred) by the end of the 1600s. Since clay—*tsuchi* or *do*—was packed tightly into straw rice bales—*tawara* or *hyo*—and placed on top of the ground to delineate the wrestling arena, the area itself soon came to be called dohyo, or "clay and rice bales." At first the bales, each containing over twenty-two gallons of earth, were placed just as they were on the ground to enclose a square or circular area, and a wrestler tripped over them and fell down if he was pushed out of the ring by his opponent. On the eastern and western sides of the ring a single bale was often removed to facili-

19. *The earliest known depiction of a dohyo made by laying out bales on the ground. Said to come from the Kofuku-ji temple in Nara. Circa 1670.*

tate entrances and exits and to provide drainage in case of rain. A square-shaped ring with pillars at the four corners was popular in the late seventeenth century in Edo, Osaka, and Kyoto. In the Nambu region of the Oshu district, rings had wooden roofs held up by the pillars, and by the middle of the eighteenth century the roofed ring was adopted for use in the major urban centers. The rice bales were made smaller by degrees and cut off at a fixed size, and by the 1720s they were being imbedded halfway into the ground.

Gondaiyu's petition also included the outlining of specific holds and throws to be used in the tournament. From mid-Muromachi, sumo techniques had been generally referred to as *shijuhatte,* or the forty-eight hands: the term did not refer to a special number but merely meant "many." (It was also common, for example, to refer to the numerous varieties of hawks, or *taka,* as the "forty-eight hawks.") However, while the known techniques of sumo had swollen from the some 100 customarily employed during the Muromachi period to over 250 by the late seventeenth century, the official *kimarite,* or defined hands, were arbitrarily set at forty-eight in the 1680s. Techniques inherited from past ages were categorized into four fundamental groups: *nage,* or throwing;

20. *Detail of a folding screen showing a square Nambu-style ring, but without a roof. Late seventeenth century.*

kake, or tripping; *sori,* or bending; and *hineri,* or twisting. For each of these, twelve of the most commonly used holds were designated, making a total of forty-eight. Later, other groupings—crushing, maneuvering, special tricks—were invented to absorb the remaining techniques.

Edicts prohibiting street-corner sumo continued to be issued periodically well into the eighteenth century, but henceforth legitimate benefit sumo was excluded from the bans. Organizers (*kanjin moto*) of the benefit tournaments were required to obtain the proper documents of permission from the shrine magistrate, and officials representing the magistrate's office attended the events to supervise the matches. Wooden planks, proclaiming with the phrase *gomen o komuru* (permission granted) that the tournaments had official sanction, were set up by the wrestling grounds. To draw up the required petitions, Gondaiyu acted as benefit-tournament organizer and became the liaison between the wrestling groups and the authorities: the permit issued to Gondaiyu in 1684 contained the title *toshiyori* (elder) that such organizers would come to adopt. Toshiyori was a term used during the Edo period to refer to statesmen in the central and provincial governments as well as to the leaders of small groups of townsmen. The sumo toshiyori

21. *Late-Edo-period woodblock-print trip-tych of a benefit-sumo tournament.* Right panel: *announcers parading the streets with a drum to advertise the tournament; kimono-clad wrestlers entering the tournament grounds; wrestlers warming up in the ring; announcer reading aloud the names of the wrestlers, which are written on the folding fan he holds; wrestlers practicing.* Middle panel: *ring-entering ceremony; the referee holding up placards with wrestlers' names written on them; the yokozuna ring-entering ceremony; referee announcing wrestlers' names before a match; eastern and western champions entering the ring.* Left panel: *bow-twirling ceremony; wrestlers in the training chamber getting ready for a match; at the entrance to the arena; the referee and judges in the ring; the referees' chamber; dividing up the profits from the tournament.*

that developed headed groups of professional wrestlers, organized and directed the benefit-sumo performances, and were responsible for keeping the tournaments free of fighting.

It is clear that the systematization of Edo sumo had already begun to take place at the time Gondaiyu and his fourteen wrestlers performed at the Fukagawa Hachiman Shrine. Although an official permit system was established in the city in 1684, between that year and 1757 the only surviving records pertaining to sumo in Edo are three wooden programs dated 1724, 1729, and 1750.

It was, however, in Osaka and Kyoto, not in Edo, that the popularization of benefit sumo was brought to fruition. The center of the entertainment culture remained in the western merchant cities until the middle of the eighteenth century, and sumo was no exception to this. Records of large benefit-sumo tournaments in Kyoto in the late sixteenth century attest to its early development in that city. By the end of the Genroku era (1688–1704), a period of affluence and decadence that witnessed the first major blossoming of the urban culture, tournaments were performed with regularity in both Kyoto and Osaka. The hierarchy of the ranks of *ozeki*, *sekiwake*, and *komusubi* were established, and *banzuke* (programs) listing the names and ranks of the wrestlers were developed.

During the Muromachi period the highest-ranking wrestlers were known as *seki,* or barriers; the term *sekimori* (barrier-defender) was common from the tenth century and was often used to denote a man of great strength. By the seventeenth century, if a wrestler defeated all of his opponents the feat was known as *seki o toru,* or to take the barrier, and hence *sekitori* came to denote a champion wrestler. From the late 1690s the highest-ranked wrestler was known as ozeki (big seki) and the second-highest as sekiwake (attendant to the seki). The final match of a tournament had been commonly known from Heian times as the *musubi,* or concluding match, and it is thought that since the third-ranked wrestlers often participated in those matches, members of that rank came to be called komusubi, or little musubi.

The earliest record of a program dates to a seven-day benefit-sumo performance at the Okazaki Tenno Shrine in Kyoto in 1699. Two wooden planks were displayed on the tournament grounds, one listing the names of the referees and wrestlers of the eastern, or benefit, team and the other, the western, or challenging, team. Originally the boards were called *mokuroku,* but from the early years of the eighteenth century the term banzuke was generally employed to refer to the lists of rankings displayed at the tourna-

ments and at the crossroads of the amusement districts to advertise the events and attract spectators. In 1717 programs began to be printed with wood blocks on rice paper: two separate sheets were issued, one for each team. The two-page programs, read horizontally from right to left, were used in Osaka and Kyoto through the end of the nineteenth century.

The enthusiasm of the provincial lords in sponsoring wrestlers had been held in check for over three decades by the repeated proscriptions against sumo, but with the emergence of professional sumo in the Genroku era, the practice was revived. During the second half of the Edo period the lords of Kishu, Izumo, Sanuki, Awa, Harima, Sendai, Tsugaru, Nambu, Shonai, Kumamoto, Satsuma, and Tosa were well known for hiring wrestlers. The term *rikishi*, or strong samurai, began to be used to refer to wrestlers around the end of the seventeenth century, and *kakae rikishi* (embraced rikishi) was used to denote a wrestler retained by a provincial lord as a vassal. These retained wrestlers were raised to the status of samurai and were permitted to carry two swords, while wrestlers who were not patronized by a daimyo could only carry a sword while traveling or for ceremonial occasions; normally these men sported only short daggers. Many of the daimyo hired men to act as scouts for potential wrestlers within their own domains and to be in charge of their training.

As benefit-sumo tournaments took place with increasing regularity in the Horie gay quarters of Osaka and the Shijo-gawara district of Kyoto in the early decades of the eighteenth century, wrestlers patronized by the provincial daimyo were invited by the sumo elders of the two cities to participate in the matches. The division of east and west teams was determined separately for each tournament, based roughly on the geographical origin of the wrestlers involved. One year wrestlers from Osaka and Sendai would make up the eastern team, with champions from Kyushu as the western team; the following year might see Osaka and Sanuki on the east, and Nambu and Akita on the west. Because the slate of wrestlers changed each year, the wrestlers of each team began to mount the ring en masse to be introduced to the crowds prior to the beginning of the matches, and a ring-entering (dohyo iri) ceremony was evolved to give the spectators some idea of each wrestler's individual prowess. The wrestlers stamped heavily on the ground—shiko, or strong leg—and clapped their hands together to show the strength of their arms. For the matches, the wrestlers wore knee-length frontal aprons embroidered with the family crest of their lords, often with elaborate fringe and silken ropes around the waist,

◁ 22. *The first vertical-style program printed on wood blocks in Edo in 1757.*

as the daimyo competed with each other to advertise the wealth of their domains through the wrestlers' *kesho mawashi,* or decorative aprons. (By the latter half of the century, because the wrestlers on occasion found their hands caught up in the long fringes of the aprons, these were relegated for use only in the ring-entering ceremonies.) Tournaments began to be held regularly twice a year in the 1740s, and popular champion wrestlers came back year after year to assume the top ranks. Often the entire slate of wrestlers traveled to Kyoto to perform upon the conclusion of a tournament in Osaka. They went to Edo as well, and in the few surviving programs of benefit sumo held there prior to 1757, the high ranks were dominated by wrestlers from Osaka.

Early Organization   Sumo in Edo was not organized to any great degree until the middle of the eighteenth century. Paper programs had been issued in Osaka and Kyoto from 1717, but it was not until forty years later that a printed program appeared in Edo. When it did, however, it was drawn up in a radically different format from the two-page horizontal program used in the western cities. A desire to cast off their subjugation to Osaka sumo led the Edo sumo elders to devise a one-page program in a vertical format for an eight-day performance at the Asakusa Kuramae Hachiman Shrine in 1757. The new program listed all of the names of the wrestlers on a single sheet, with the eastern wrestlers on the right and the western wrestlers on the left. An obvious advantage of the new program was that it made the relative status of the wrestlers of both teams immediately apparent. This first program had seven rows, but in 1761 a five-row program was adopted. To fit all of the names in the shortened program, the print was made smaller as the rows progressed down the page. A six-row program was experimented with briefly in 1769, but the elders reverted to using five rows at the next tournament, a format that is still used today. A system of ranking, based on the number of rows on the program, was evolved. Those wrestlers listed in the top row of the program, which consisted of the *sanyaku,* the three highest ranks (ozeki, sekiwake, and komusubi) and the highest in status of the *maegashira* wrestlers (maegashira referring generally to all wrestlers below the top ranks) were known collectively as *makuuchi,* a term said to have originated in the custom of having high-ranking wrestlers sit behind a curtain (*maku*) near the wrestling ring. (See page 138.) Wrestlers below the rank of makuuchi came to be known as *makushita* (below the maku), although they also drew appellations from their positions on the program. Those whose names were listed in

23. *Woodblock-print triptych of sumo performed at the Eko-in in the Ryogoku district of Edo. Mid-Edo period.*

the second row of the program became *nidamme* (second row) and those in the third row, *sandamme* (third row). Because of superstition regarding the word *shi,* which means both four and death, wrestlers listed in the fourth row of the program came to be known as *jonidan,* originally written with the character *jo,* meaning upper and referring to the second row up from the bottom. The last row was known as *jonokuchi,* or entrance to jo. Wrestlers of this rank, being the lowest in status of all those listed in the program, had their names written in extremely fine print.

From 1757 tournaments began to be held regularly in the third and tenth months of the lunar year. In 1761 sumo in Edo took on the name kanjin-ozumo, or benefit grand sumo. Performances, known as the spring and winter *basho* (sites), spanned eight or ten clear days—these outdoor tournaments would not be concluded until that number of non-rainy days had passed—in temporary open-air theaters erected on the grounds of temples or shrines: the theaters during the latter part of the Edo period were often capable of seating up to 3,000 spectators. The wrestling grounds were enclosed by high wooden walls set with double-tiered covered balconies reached by bamboo ladders. Large wooden entrance gates were set up, and *chaya,* or teahouses, were erected nearby to cater to the crowds. The ring was in the very center of the theater,

24. *The scaffold and drum at the Eko-in, looking across the Sumida River toward Mount Fuji. From a nineteenth-century woodblock print by Hiroshige.*

a square raised platform covered by a wooden roof supported by four pillars. Around it, and extending out to the balconies, were box seats delineated by hemp ropes.

During the late Muromachi period, wrestling matches had been performed in shrines in areas enclosed by curtains. As in early Kabuki and puppet-theater performances, a low-set scaffolding (*yagura*) was erected over the entranceway. A drum set on a platform at the top of the scaffolding and surrounded by bunting was beaten to announce the beginning of the shrine entertainments. When the grounds of the Eko-in temple in Ryogoku began to be used for sumo tournaments in the late eighteenth century, the scaffolding was removed from its place over the entrance gates. Instead, a tall scaffolding approximately sixteen meters in height was constructed near the approach to the nearby Higashi Ryogoku Bridge, where the sound of the drum beaten at dawn on each day of a tournament traveled far down the Sumida River. While scaffolding had originally been used for other theatrical performances, during the mid-Edo period the Tokugawa authorities forbade

25. The sumo grounds at the Eko-in temple around 1850. In the upper right panel is the Ryogoku Bridge over the Sumida River, with the teahouses pictured below it and the sumo arena in the left panel. Woodblock-print triptych by Kunisato.

its use except as lookout towers for the shogun's falcons, fire watch-towers, and announcement-drum towers for sumo performances.

Groups of men were also hired to parade the streets of the city carrying large announcement drums. Starting early in the morning prior to the first day of a tournament, these men walked through the Shitamachi, Fukagawa, Shinagawa, Yamanote, and Asakusa districts of Edo to announce the matches of the following day.

Most tournaments took place in the large temples of the more sparsely populated eastern sectors of Edo. Between 1757 and 1780 most of the eight-day tournaments were held at the Fukagawa Hachiman Shrine. Ten-day performances were established in 1778, and from that time until the beginning of the twentieth century most tournaments were held at the Eko-in temple in Ryogoku. The Eko-in was constructed after a devastating fire destroyed nearly half the city and killed over 100,000 people in 1657; the temple's grounds had been chosen for the mass interment of the ashes of the dead from that disaster. To fund the temple, a section of its compounds was set aside to be rented out as an entertainment site. Most sumo tournaments in Edo were held at the Eko-in by the late eighteenth century, and in 1833 the site was officially established as the *hombasho*, or home site, of Edo sumo.

In 1684 the masterless samurai who acted as the organizers of loose coalitions of wrestlers for performances of benefit sumo had been given the title of elder (toshiyori) by the shrine magistrate of Edo. The elders (*totori* in Osaka and Kyoto) handled the business end of benefit-sumo tournaments, acting as liaison with government officials to obtain permits for the performances, organizing the city's wrestlers, and making arrangements with the provincial lords for the appearance at the tournaments of the wrestlers they retained. In 1719 a directive was issued by the Edo authorities specifying that only "professional" wrestlers and organizers could take part in benefit-sumo performances. While the early elders had often been unemployed samurai, after 1719 virtually all of the elders emerged from the ranks of retired wrestlers. In the 1720s there were ten sumo elders in Edo. By 1780 there were thirty, and at the end of the century the number grew to thirty-eight. The elders held their positions until death or retirement from the sumo world. The two most important elders were the benefit-sumo organizer and his assistant. Similar organizations developed in Osaka, Kyoto, and Nagoya during the early eighteenth century.

The duties of the sumo elders were not limited to the staging of tournaments and establishing liaison with the sumo organizations of the other cities but included the training of novice wrestlers. Many retired champions became elders and established *heya*, or stables, of disciples in their residences in Edo. It became customary for the elder of a stable to pass on his assumed name to a promising disciple, who would then inherit both the stable and his master's position as a sumo elder. Nearly all of the Edo *sumo-beya* (sumo stables) were founded between 1751 and 1781.

The emergence of the supremacy of the Edo sumo association (*sumo kaisho*) over the wrestling groups of Osaka, Kyoto, and the provinces in the second half of the eighteenth century was one of the main factors leading to the great popularity of Edo sumo in the 1780s. During this period Edo came to be recognized as the new cultural capital of the country, and as sumo began to prosper, the Edo sumo world became increasingly systematized. The strict exclusivity of the Edo sumo elders meant that wrestlers who came from outside the city were invariably assigned to the lowest positions of rank when combined sumo tournaments were held. As a result, wrestlers retained by the provincial daimyo began to enter the stables of the Edo elders, and even wrestlers who were already

26. *Wrestlers and spectators crammed around the ring during a tournament. Late-Edo-period scroll by Matora.*

apprenticed to retired masters in Osaka or Kyoto migrated to Edo to join the stable of a master there. From around 1770 the Edo benefit-sumo organization completely dominated the course of sumo across the country.

Professional *gyoji*, or referees, who founded their own stables and held positions as elders, first appeared in the late seventeenth century. The term gyoji (written with the characters meaning function things) dates to the Heian period, when refereeing was done by the tachiawase. Even at that time, however, there was a position known as gyoji that was assigned to a courtier of the sixth rank, who was put in charge of miscellaneous duties pertaining to the sumo ceremonies of the court. The duties of the early gyoji were assumed by a *sumo bugyo*, or sumo magistrate, for the matches performed for the early Kamakura shoguns in the late twelfth and early thirteenth centuries. These men also acted as referees. By the early Muromachi period the term gyoji was adopted by the samurai who acted as temporary judges for wrestling matches between warriors. In 1570 two gyoji officials, the warriors Kise Taro Dayu and Kise Zoshun'an, were appointed by Oda Nobunaga to direct his great sumo tournaments.

When sumo was restricted by the Edo authorities to performances on shrine precincts in 1684, professional benefit-sumo tournaments began to adopt Shinto purification rituals common to the ceremonies of god-service sumo. The ring came to be regarded as a sacred battlefield, and great importance was placed on spiritually preparing the arena and the wrestlers for the matches. Salt, which had been used in ancient Shinto practices as a purifying substance, was thrown onto the ring by the wrestlers and dabbed onto their tongues to drive away evil spirits. The ring-entering ceremony, which first appeared in illustrations dating to the early decades of the eighteenth century, adopted the Shinto rituals of clapping the hands to attract the attention of the deities and stamping the feet to drive away malignant spirits; at the same time, these actions gave the spectators a chance to view the strength of the wrestlers prior to the matches.

As sumo took on traditional Shinto elements, the referees, as the overseers of the performance, assumed the roles of surrogate Shinto priests. Official licensing to perform their duties became important, and the authority to issue such permits came to be controlled by the Yoshida and Gojo families. Even before the Edo period it had been customary for the provincial lords and military commanders who retained men of the martial arts among their vassals to appoint special officials to take charge of their training. The most prominent of the early sumo officials was the noble Gojo family of Kyoto, who claimed descent from the legendary Nomi no Sukune and who emerged during the late Muromachi period. The Gojos, a branch of the Sugawara family that had been founded in the late Kamakura period, excelled in belles-lettres, and their initial connection with sumo is not clear. As patron nobles of the sumo world, the Gojos became a symbol of authority, and aspiring sumo officials tended to seek them out in order to gain their recognition. One such petitioner became the founder of the Yoshida family, which was to become the most important line of hereditary sumo officials.

The name Yoshida Oikaze appeared as a referee in the earliest reference to a written program in 1699 in Kyoto. With the patronage of the wealthy Hosokawa lords of Kumamoto and the sponsorship of the Nijo family of nobles in Kyoto, Yoshida Oikaze gradually accumulated power and influence over the other hereditary referee families, and by the early eighteenth century the Yoshidas rose to undisputed prominence as the principal hereditary line of referees. In 1726 the referee Kimura Shonosuke sought official recognition from the Yoshidas as a disciple, and he was followed in 1729 by Shikimori Godaiyu. Both were to found hereditary lines as the major referees of Edo, although the main Shikimori line changed its name to Kinosuke in 1765. A list of referees recognized as disciples of the Yoshida family around 1770 included Kimura and Shikimori in Edo, Iwai Sauma in Kyoto, Shakushi Ichigaku in Osaka, Hattori Shikiemon in Higo, and Suminoe Shikikuro in Nagasaki. Only the Nagase family of sumo referees remained completely independent of the Yoshida officials, but they never gained prominence outside of their home province of Oshu.

The role of the referee began to undergo changes in the first half of the eighteenth century. As sumo performances became more systematized, the *shikiri*, or position taken by a wrestler at the start of a match, was evolved, and the referees began to use their *gumbai uchiwa* (war fans) to signal the start of a match. The traditional ceremonial dress of the samurai was adopted as the referee's costume.

The early announcers (*yobidashi*) were not clearly differentiated from the ranks of the referees. Until around 1750 the officials who announced the names and home provinces of the wrestlers as they ascended the ring were called *mae gyoji*, or preceding referees. Later the names *fure* or *nanori*, both meaning announcer, were popularly used to refer to these officials. They were also known as *tsubaki gyoji*, or squatting referees, because they preceded the wrestlers into the ring and sat down on their heels in the center as they called out the names of the wrestlers. The name yobidashi (calling out) appeared near the end of the century.

Originally the duties of the referees included the judging of matches, but as sumo became more popular and the outcome of the matches more important to the various daimyo who sponsored the champion wrestlers, complaints regarding the decision of the contests were increasingly common. In such cases the referee consulted with the sumo elders, who watched the wrestling from seats just below the ring. From about 1780 four elders began to sit on the platform itself, with their backs against the pillars around the ring. Formally known as *naka aratame*, or ascertainers in the middle, the judges were popularly called the *shihom-bashira*, or the four pillars.

As the biannual tournaments in Edo grew in popularity, samurai who were permanently quartered in the daimyo mansions there began to represent their lords at the benefit-sumo matches in order to report on the performances of vassal wrestlers and to scout the lower ranks of the wrestlers for potential champions. Wrestlers with promise were invited to call at the daimyo mansion in Edo as *odeiri rikishi*, or visiting wrestlers. As proof of their somewhat nebulous relationship with the lords, they were awarded a decorative skirt with the family crest of the domain and were introduced at the tournaments as vassals of their particular lord, but apart from that, the relationship was purely nominal. If a wrestler's subsequent record was good enough, however, he stood a chance of being awarded samurai status and a salary from the daimyo. During the late Edo period an upper-ranking wrestler supported by a daimyo lord received a stipend of about twenty *koku*—one koku being approximately 45 gallons, or the amount of rice consumed by one person in a year—while those below makuuchi rank received only about five koku. Generous traveling allowances were given to wrestlers during their tours of the provinces, and additional awards of cash were made when the wrestlers participated in the tournaments in Edo.

Wrestlers who had no patrons were forced to depend largely on the salaries they made at each performance. The income of the Edo tournaments was supervised by the benefit-sumo organizer and his assistant. Any profit left after the liquidating of expenses and the salaries of the elders and wrestlers remained in the hands of these two men, who gave lump sums to the masters of the stables for them, in turn, to distribute to their disciples. Wrestlers were also supplied with food by the elders for the duration of each tournament, and sometimes spectators threw expensive articles of clothing into the ring as a congratulatory gesture for the winner of a match.

All of the wrestlers who participated in the Edo tournaments joined the stable of one of the Edo elders, but those wrestlers who were retained by a daimyo had to be officially "borrowed" from the provincial overlords in order for them to appear. To keep in good favor with the various daimyo, the elders went to great pains in the compilation of the programs, for a lord who was dissatisfied with the ranking or choice of opponent assigned to his wrestlers could simply withdraw his permission for them to perform. Samurai representing the daimyo sat near the ring to watch the matches, and if there was the slightest doubt in a decision called against a vassal wrestler, it was the duty of the warrior to protest the decision. When complaints were serious enough—and the lord powerful enough—negotiations between the samurai and the sumo elders continued long after the conclusion of the tournament. Such incidents occurred with increasing frequency near the end of the Edo period. To avoid volatile confrontations, many matches involving retained wrestlers were called as draws, or decisions were deferred altogether.

The decade of the 1780s witnessed widespread famine and

27. *Playing cards (center) with a sumo motif, by Shun'ei. Printed around 1784.*

epidemics in the provinces and corruption and a continued decline in the economic solvency of the central government. For the merchant class, however, it was a period of continuous prosperity. Refugees from the disasters of the countryside poured into Edo, where destitute women were often forced to enter the countless houses of prostitution that sprang up in the entertainment districts. At the same time, urban culture flourished, and Kabuki saw a major revival. The values of the merchant class began to be conspicuously reflected in both literature and art, as books dealing humorously with the daily life of the populace appeared with increasing frequency, while the art of the *ukiyo-e* woodblock print was brought to perfection by the great artists who produced the likenesses of famous actors and the courtesans of the gay quarters. During the final decades of the eighteenth century, champion wrestlers joined the ranks of the actors and prostitutes as the popular heroes of the merchant class. Incidents involving wrestlers became the ribald subject matter both of comical poetry and of a type of mass-produced book known as *kibyoshi*, or yellow covers. Woodblock prints depicting the massive features of the favorite Edo champions were widely distributed, and even sumo dolls and playing cards with sumo motifs were popular.

Although champion wrestlers began to appear in succession, the Edo sumo elders sought to appeal to the degenerate tastes of the "floating world" of the townsmen by employing giants or overgrown children to participate in the ring-entering ceremonies of the tournaments. These feature wrestlers were given the rank of ozeki, although only on rare occasions did they show any prowess as wrestlers, and they almost never participated in any of the matches. Known as *kamban ozeki* (billboard champions), these attractions often were seen at only one or two tournaments and were then replaced by new feature wrestlers.

Codification   The story behind the creation of the yokozuna status is complicated. Under the tenth shogun, Ieharu, the central government had been dominated by the corrupting influence of the statesman Tanuma Okitsugu. When Ieharu died in 1786, Okitsugu was dismissed and replaced by Matsudaira Sadanobu, a bureaucratic official who took over the reins of the Tokugawa government as the guardian of the young shogun Ienari. Before Ienari came of age in 1793, Sadanobu issued a number of reforms to try to stem the rapid decline of public morals in Edo. The many activities—including sumo—of the amusement districts came under close scrutiny. To ward off a major repetition of the disastrous events of the mid-seventeenth century, the Edo sumo elders set about making benefit sumo more respectable. In 1789, in response to edicts requiring the documentation of precedent for certain activities and offices, Yoshida Oikaze, who had come to hold a major position of authority in Edo sumo, made a bold play for power by submitting to the shrine magistrate of Edo a number documents substantiating both his own authority over the sumo world and the supposed history of some of the sumo traditions.

In his lineage chart, Oikaze claimed descent from a warrior by the name of Yoshida Ietsuru of Echizen Province. The earliest family of referees, he said, was the line of Shiga no Seirin, appointed by the emperor Shomu as the official Heian-court referee in the early eighth century. When no descendant of Seirin could by found in the late twelfth century, Ietsuru was selected by the emperor Gotoba to act as the referee for the last of the tournament-banquet ceremonies. His name was changed to Oikaze, and he was given a war fan with which to direct the matches. Five centuries later, Oikaze's history continued, when the shogun Tsuneyoshi was touring Higo Province in Kyushu, he viewed sumo, refereed by the then current Yoshida Oikaze. The shogun was so impressed by the man's performance that he allowed one of his own vassals to become a disciple of the Yoshida family and declared that the licensing of referees and wrestlers from that day forth would be done solely by a Yoshida.

Included among the practices that the Yoshida officials supposedly controlled the licensing of was an account of the origin of the yokozuna, the rope of plaited silk worn around the waists of certain wrestlers during pre-match ceremonies. According to Oikaze, there was a great wrestler in the early ninth century by the name of Hajikami of Omi Province. Once when he was performing ritual sumo at the Sumiyoshi Shrine in Settsu Province he so outmatched the other wrestlers that the referee, Shiga no Seirin, took the large sacred rope (*shimenawa*) from the front of the shrine and wrapped it around Hajikami's waist, proclaiming that if any wrestler could place his hands on the rope, Hajikami would be declared the loser. Seirin set the wrestlers at each other once more, but even so there was not a single man who could make contact with the rope.

According to the Yoshida document—and one written fifteen years earlier in an account of the origins of the Gojo family by the referee Shikimori Godayu—it was common practice well before the eighteenth century for one or two of the strongest wrestlers of the time to participate in the ground-breaking ceremonies preceding the construction of castles or great mansions. During the course of the ritual, straw ropes were laid on the ground, and over those yokozuna, or horizontal ropes, a wrestler performed rites of exorcism, stamping his feet hard on the ground to drive off evil deities. To purify his own body, the wrestler wore a shimenawa, which was traditionally hung in front of shrines as a symbol of the divine activities of the guardian Shinto deities of production. For those occasions a special license was granted to the wrestlers to testify to their indoctrination in the secrets necessary for the ritual. In 1773 the Shikimori referee attributed that licensing to the Gojo family of sumo officials in Kyoto. But in the history of the Yoshida family in 1789 Oikaze claimed that the secrets of the ritual had been transferred to them as well.

Actually it had been popular among wrestlers, especially in Osaka and Kyoto, to bind ropes of black and white silk around the waists of their decorative frontal skirts from the late seventeenth century. By the middle of the eighteenth century, the Gojo sumo officials began to issue permits to popular wrestlers to wear such decorations, and it was at that time that the story about the secret ritual was invented. No reference to any such custom is mentioned in any Edo-period documents except the histories of the Gojo and

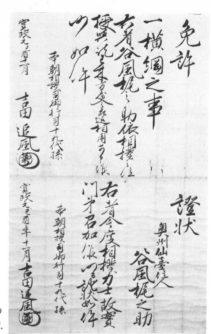

28. *The yokozuna license issued to Tanikaze by Yoshida Oikaze in 1789.*

Yoshida families. By 1789, however, Yoshida Oikaze saw the licensing power of the Gojo family as a threat to his absolute control over the sumo world; so along with his family history he included a petition to the Edo authorities for the official recognition of his own power to issue what he called, for the first time, the *yokozuna menkyo,* or yokozuna license.

Oikaze's petitions were accepted, and in 1789 he was recognized by the Edo authorities as the "official of the court sumo." Just prior to the tournament of the eleventh month in that year he issued yokozuna licenses to the champions Tanikaze Kajinosuke and Onogawa Kisaburo, and ten days later Tanikaze performed the first yokozuna ring-entering ceremony in the precincts of the Fukagawa Hachiman Shrine. The power of the Yoshida family was officially established, but the Gojo family continued to be known as the "main house of sumo" for well over a century, and it became customary for the yokozuna licenses to be issued jointly by both lines. The term yokozuna, which originally referred to the certification of a champion wrestler to perform the yokozuna ring-entering ceremony, eventually came to mean the wrestler himself. It was not made into a rank, however, until 1909.

So well did Oikaze succeed in imparting a respectable history to sumo that in 1791 a sumo tournament was held in the Fukiage gardens of Edo Castle. Ostensibly a part of the official Tokugawa policy to encourage the martial arts, the performance was held primarily to permit the twenty-one year old shogun Ienari to witness a match between the two great sumo heroes of the day, Tanikaze and Onogawa. Shogunal sumo lifted the sport out of the vulgar world of entertainment and imparted to it a sense of ritual that later became its major characteristic. To equal the honor of the occasion, the Edo sumo elders, led by Yoshida Oikaze, set down refined rules and rituals that had been slowly developing for benefit sumo during the preceding century. In keeping with a prevailing interest in Shinto learning and tradition, a number of customs that had lain dormant since the days of the Heian-court tournament-banquets were researched and revived, and an elaborate ring-purifying ceremony was devised to precede the matches. The ring itself, which had been viewed as a sacred area since the first infusion of god-service sumo practices into professional sumo in the late seventeenth century, was redesigned and given an extremely complex symbolic mélange of Shinto, Buddhist, and Confucian precepts. In explaining the symbolism of the ring, a contemporary source stated:

> The four pillars of the ring are based on the *I Ching* [Book of Changes]. The inner ring is the *t'ai chi* [the realm of the absolute]. The entrances on the left and right represent the yin and yang. The four pillars represent the four seasons, and with the earth at the center representing the five elements [metal, water, wood, fire, earth] as well as the five virtues of Confucianism [benevolence, justice, ritual, wisdom, faith]. The curtain stretching from the north pillar clockwise around the top consists of tricolored silk of black, red, and yellow, the purpose of which is to purify the hearts of the entering and exiting wrestlers. The north pillar is called the *gokuin* [northern extremity], although in benefit sumo it is called the *yaku-bashira* [the pillar of the head judge]. The rice sacks that form the ring symbolize the ritual of harvesting the five grains [rice, wheat, barley, millet, beans]. Although *joran-zumo* [sumo viewed by the shogun] and benefit sumo are different in status and form, they agree in principal and follow the concepts of the *I Ching.* . . .[3]

The 1791 tournament in front of the shogun at Edo Castle was not without its tensions. In those days—and indeed, up through the early twentieth century—it was common for wrestlers to delay the

29. *Tanikaze and Onogawa wrestling in a tournament in Edo. Eighteenth-century wood-block print by Shunsho.*

beginning of a match for a considerable period of time, each waiting for the psychologically correct moment to attack his opponent. In order to include all the wrestlers retained by all the daimyo in the 1791 tournament, however, strict time limits were imposed for the starts. This caused no small confusion and anxiety among the wrestlers, who were already nervous about the prospect of appearing before the shogun.

The indisputable high point of the tournament was the match between Tanikaze and Onogawa, who were the last of the 164 wrestlers to perform, and a minor uproar arose throughout Edo over the outcome of this match between the two yokozuna champions. Yoshida Oikaze was the referee for the match, and just before he raised his fan to start the contest, Tanikaze charged at his rival. With this, the judges ordered the match to be repeated. The second time Tanikaze moved at the very instant Oikaze motioned for the start, and Onogawa was so surprised that he was pushed backward several steps before he started to pull himself upright. Seeing this display, Oikaze stopped the match and pointed his fan at Tanikaze,

declaring Onogawa the loser because of his lack of attention and Tanikaze the victor of the tournament.

Tanikaze, Onogawa, and Raiden　Tanikaze Kajinosuke, the son of a humble farmer from northern Japan, was unquestionably one of the great sumo heroes of all time. So strong was his contemporary reputation that it was said of him: "No Tanikaze before Tanikaze, and no Tanikaze after Tanikaze." In fact, however, there *was* another Tanikaze before Tanikaze, a wrestler by the name of Tanikaze Kajinosuke from Takamatsu, who in the early decades of the eighteenth century remained undefeated in the sumo tournaments of Osaka for a reported nine consecutive years. The first Tanikaze was apparently a great wrestler, and forty or fifty years later the future Tanikaze, wrestling under the name Dategaseki, heard of him and adopted the same name.

Tanikaze Kajinosuke was born Kinji Yoshiro in 1750 in the village of Kasumimine (present-day Kasumine) in the Oshu district. At the age of nineteen he went to Edo to become a wrestler, training under the elder Sekinoto Okuemon of Sendai. At first he took the name Hidenoyama, which he later changed to Dategaseki Yoshiro, then to Dategaseki Moriemon, and in 1776 finally to Tanikaze Kajinosuke. In 1789 Tanikaze, along with the wrestler Onogawa, was given a yokozuna license by Yoshida Oikaze. Two years later he confronted his rival, Onogawa, in front of the shogun. In his entire career it is said that he lost only fourteen times in a total of forty-four tournaments. For one span of four years it is recorded that he fought with sixty-three successive victories.

Tanikaze became a living legend, and the many comic exploits, both real and attributed, associated with him became topics for eighteenth-century writers. In 1784, the year that Tanikaze first lost to Onogawa, there was one sumo enthusiast who preferred sumo above all else. On the day that Tanikaze and Onogawa were to compete, this fan went early so as to get a good seat. He favored Onogawa, and when Onogawa won, pushing Tanikaze out of the ring with no apparent effort at all, the entire audience rose with a great yell. The sumo fan was so excited that he threw his coat, haori, and even his sash into the ring, leaving the theater entirely naked. On the way home he met an acquaintance, who, seeing him, exclaimed: "My goodness, your favorite must have lost!" (That is, "You must have lost the shirt off your back in betting.") The naked sumo enthusiast replied: "No, no, no, no—I lost my clothes because he won!" Throwing clothes into the ring was a common congratulatory gesture, and the winning wrestler would usually send his underlings out the next day to redeem the articles for cash.

In one yellow journal dated 1792, Tanikaze is referred to as Onikaze:

> The wrestler by the name of Onikaze, who had been known for being undefeated, was under discussion.
> "No, no . . . even Onikaze is said to have been thrown down yesterday."
> "Who did he lose to?"
> "He was thrown down by Agemaki."
> "I never heard of a wrestler by that name. Where was the wrestler from?"
> "Well . . . actually it was just a prostitute from the Miura-ya."[4]

Another anecdote comes from one of the miscellaneous collections (*zuihitsu*) of the period:

30. *Tanikaze pictured with one of the "Three Beauties" of Edo, by Shuncho, a woodblock-print artist who specialized in drawing famous courtesans.*

For whatever reason, one day Tanikaze was very upset with one of his disciples. Taking him aside, he yelled in a loud voice that he should be beaten to death. Tanikaze was at this time in a house of prostitution in the entertainment district. All the other disciples went in turn to the house to apologize for their unfortunate comrade, but Tanikaze refused to accept any apology and further said angrily that anyone who meddled in the matter would be beaten to death as well. No one dared go near him. One of his disciples, however, who was endowed with some wit, devised to bring in Tanikaze's young mistress, who was around seventeen years of age, and he asked her to humor Tanikaze and bring him out. The girl accepted and, going into the house, took Tanikaze's hands and asked for forgiveness for all of his disciples, and begged him to return.

Upon this Tanikaze said: "All right, all right," and came out of the house, led by the young girl, and things settled down.

Later on the disciples all remarked to each other: "The

united strength of this many wrestlers does not even come near that of a young lady." And everyone was deeply impressed by the wit of this disciple.[5]

In 1800, five years after Tanikaze's death, another view of the bulky Tanikaze was published:

> Tanikaze said, somewhat sadly, to his wife: "Oi, old woman. To have been born with a figure like this, I am handicapped. I have never even seen my own navel."
> His wife said: "Try taking a peek. I can give you a hand." And she began to help him. Tanikaze was embarrassed, but bent over. His wife said: "Bend over some more. It's farther."
> Saying this, she pushed down on his head, but Tanikaze said: "Oh, it's too embarrassing. Let's give up."
> His wife only replied: "Bend over a little bit more." And she kept pushing on Tanikaze's head. Tanikaze then bent over a little too far and fell, rolling over onto his back. His wife, lifting her arms wide, said: "Haa! I threw you!"[6]

Tanikaze retired from sumo in 1794 and returned to his native village, where he contracted influenza the following year and died at the age of forty-five. The wrestler was by that time so well known that for years after his death it was said that when the people of Edo caught a cold (*kaze*) they remembered the fate of the strong wrestler Tani*kaze* and became frightened.

The rivalry between Tanikaze and Onogawa Kisaburo, which began in the early 1780s with Onogawa's surprise victory over the champion, escalated the popularity of both the wrestlers themselves and sumo as a whole. For the audience the contest between east and west as represented by Tanikaze and Onogawa invariably created a great amount of anticipation before the matches. In fact, on days when the two were to confront each other the excitement at the entrance gates was so intense that on at least one occasion in Kyoto people were trampled to death in the jostling crowds waiting outside the tournament grounds.

Onogawa was born in 1758 in Omi Province, and at fifteen he became the disciple of Onogawa Saisuke, an elder in Osaka. The young wrestler, who originally went by the name of Sagamigawa Kisaburo, was later adopted by his master and changed his name to Onogawa Kisaburo. At twenty-one he left Osaka for Edo, where he was hired by the lord of Arima. Four years later Onogawa overthrew the standing champion, Tanikaze, and from that time until the latter's retirement in 1794 the two matched each other almost exactly in wins and losses. In 1789 both he and Tanikaze were licensed as yokozuna and were permitted to use the imperial color, purple, for their loincloths. Except for the four times he was beaten by Tanikaze and the two times he lost to Tanikaze's successor, Raiden, Onogawa from that time on lost no other match. On the death of his old rival in 1795, the contest against Onogawa was taken up by Raiden. After suffering two defeats at the hands of this new rival, Onogawa retired at the age of thirty-six, returning to Osaka to become an elder. He died there in 1806.

Raiden Tame-emon succeeded Tanikaze as the ozeki of the east, and from that time until his own retirement in 1810 Raiden faced eleven different ozeki of the west. Only once in that entire period was he defeated. Raiden was born Seki Tarokichi in Shinshu Province in 1767. His father was a tenant farmer who was supposedly active in god-ritual sumo. Because of his great size and power, Raiden attracted the attention of the village headman, who gave the youth his first instruction in sumo. When he was seventeen, Raiden became a disciple of the wrestler Urakaze, who noticed him while on tour in the provinces. After leaving home to train in Edo, Raiden was hired by Matsudaira Harusato, the lord of Izumo, and was given a yearly stipend of rice. It was at that time that he began to call himself Raiden. The two characters in that name—*rai* (thunder) and *den* (lightning)—were related to the character for "cloud" used in writing "Izumo," and the name was probably chosen by his patron. In the spring of 1790 Raiden accompanied his lord to Edo. The following year he participated in the sumo tournament at Edo Castle before the shogun as the sekiwake wrestler of the eastern team. The chronicles of the event note that his fame "surpasses the roaring of thunder." On the death of Tanikaze he was promoted to ozeki and remained in that position for fifteen years.

Raiden's superhuman strength was such that his opponents petitioned the elders of Edo sumo to prohibit his use of slapping— his hands were exceptionally large—and two other difficult techniques. He was never awarded the status of yokozuna, however. Some say that this was because he was involved in the murder of a rival; others think that it was because such licenses were only awarded in anticipation of a performance for the shogun. There seems to be no basis for the first theory, though, and Tanikaze and Onogawa were given their licenses eighteen months before the 1791 shogunal sumo was even proposed. It appears more likely that the Yoshida family deigned to favor wrestlers who were retained by

31. Raiden and the wrestler Jimmaku grappling in the early nineteenth century. Shun'ei.

non-Tokugawa-family daimyo, like their own lords, the Hosokawas, and did not wish to publicly ally themselves with a wrestler who, like Raiden, was retained by one of the Tokugawa Matsudaira collateral families. Inazuma Raigoro, who was later retained as a wrestler by the same Matsudaira lord of Izumo, was given a yokozuna license in 1829 by the Gojo family alone, and it was only two years afterward that the Yoshidas finally consented to confirm the title. All of the other yokozuna of the late Edo period came without exception from non-Tokugawa domains.

Raiden kept detailed notebooks throughout his career as a wrestler, and these show him traveling the length and breadth of Japan over and over again as he toured the provinces when not required by his lord to be in Izumo or by tournaments to be in Edo. A typical tour of the northern regions of the country took him to Shiraishi, Yamagata, Shibahashi, Akita, Kubota, Tsuruoka, Shirakawa, Kurohane, Utsunomiya, and Sendai. A trip to the west would see him in Hiroshima, Kokura, Saga, Shimabara, Nerihaya, and Nagasaki. Once in 1802 when in Nagasaki, he won a drinking contest with a renowned Chinese scholar by the name of Chen

Ching-shan, who presented the wrestler with calligraphy and paintings of his own (now preserved at the Hodo-ji temple in the Akasaka district of Tokyo, where Raiden's remains are buried). On his way to Shinshu the following year he performed sumo in a purification ceremony to drive away a contagious disease that was plaguing a village through which he happened to be passing. In 1804 he held a sumo exhibition to honor the first Tango no Sekku (Boys' Day, on the fifth day of the fifth month) of the young son of the lord of Marugame. In Sendai he paid homage to the tomb of Tanikaze, and in Yujima he made good debts that his late master, Urakaze, had incurred. Even after his retirement in 1811 and his appointment as an elder in Edo, Raiden continued to travel, taking his apprentice wrestlers on provincial tours, although he limited his own appearances to ring-entering ceremonies. It was only at the age of fifty, in 1816, that he finally quit his wanderings. In 1825 he died in Edo.

Raiden's popularity continued long past his death. Twenty-seven years after the wrestler passed away, a memorial stele was erected in his home village, with an inscription composed and written out by the famed scholar-calligrapher Sakuma Shozan. Raiden worship became so strong a cult that people traveled great distances to see the stele, chipping at it piecemeal and taking the bits as talismans. Eventually the original stele lost its shape entirely. During the Meiji era (1868–1912) another was erected, but Raiden's memory lived on, and the new stele succumbed to the same fate as that of its predecessor.

Decline in Late Edo　None of the wrestlers who followed could equal the popularity and magnetism of the earlier generation of Tanikaze, Onogawa, and Raiden. After Raiden retired in 1811 and the ozeki Kashiwado Shugoro in 1813, the Edo sumo elders found it once again necessary to promote billboard ozeki to attract audiences. Sumo was held again in 1794, 1802, 1823, and 1830 before the shogun Ienari, and in 1843 and 1849 tournaments were performed for his successor, Ieyoshi. In 1828 Onomatsu Midorinosuke, who was born the son of a *konnyaku* (arrowroot cake) merchant in Nodo and who originally wrestled under the name Koyanagi, was granted the license for yokozuna at the age of thirty-eight. The same year Inazuma Raigoro was appointed yokozuna by the Gojo family in Kyoto and was formally ratified in that position by the Yoshida officials two years later. For a while these two yokozuna were pitted against each other before the crowds of Edo.

As the feudal system began to visibly crumble during the Tempo era (1833–44), very few famous wrestlers stepped out into the ring, and sumo, reflecting the gloomy outlook of society, dropped in popularity. In 1843 a forty-year-old wrestler by the name of Shiranui Dakuemon, a retainer of the Kumamoto lord, was promoted to yokozuna, but he was such a bad wrestler that he was dropped back to sekiwake status for the following tournament. Hidenoyama Raigoro, after wrestling in Edo for fourteen years, became a yokozuna in 1845 and was challenged by such wrestlers as Arauma, Koyanagi, Miyoki, and Kagamigawa. The financial operation of the tournaments, however, became increasingly difficult.

In the final years of the Edo period, Unryu Hisakichi was licensed as yokozuna. Three years later, in 1864, another wrestler, Shiranui Koemon, was appointed yokozuna, and in 1867 still another, Jimmaku Kyugoro, also received that status. Because of the chaos of the civil warfare of the time, which led a year later to the Meiji Restoration, Jimmaku, who was a particularly strong wrestler, retired after participating in only one tournament as a yokozuna, leaving for Osaka to become a sumo elder. In the quickening pace of the new era and the uproar and confusion of Edo as old institutions tumbled in rapid succession, the last thing the people were interested in was wrestling.

Women's Sumo and One-Man Sumo Sumo became such a popular entertainment in the eighteenth century that it began to be caricatured with eccentric performances. *Onna-zumo*, or women's sumo, was performed as an entertainment in the houses of prostitution in Osaka's gay quarters during the Genroku era, but by the middle of the eighteenth century it had become a popular attraction. Farcical matches were staged both between women and between blind men in Edo from around 1744, and by the 1760s there emerged combined wrestling between the two. Such fights drew sizable crowds in both Edo and Osaka. One such show at the Asakusa Temple in Edo was closed down by the authorities on the grounds that it was immoral, but the exhibitions continued to be staged between women and blind men through the end of the Edo period. The women wrestlers' names, satirizing the *rikishi mei* (another term used to mean assumed wrestling names) of the professional male wrestlers, were often quite erotic: Tamanokoshi (Holder of the Balls), Chichigahari (Big Boobs), Harayagura (Watchtower on the Loins), Anagafuchi (Deep Crevice), Kaigazato (Where the Clam Lives), and so on. The advertising was equally suggestive: "Blind search for a dark spot! Mutual groping and

32. *Near the end of the Edo period, huge female wrestlers enlivened the entertain-* ▷
ment districts with ribald women's sumo.

search, especially the woman's way as it is well known in *that* technique, as soft as willow branches swaying in the wind, exhausting all the techniques! All will be revealed!"[7]

An edict in 1873 prohibited wrestling matches between women and blind men, but wrestling between women continued to be performed. Around the middle of the Meiji era women's sumo was presented at the Eko-in, but no sooner had it opened than it was closed down by the authorities: it was decreed that women could no longer wrestle, although lifting weights was permissible. The women wrestlers retreated to Yamagata Prefecture in northern Japan, and, clad in both upper and lower garments, they began to perform on the provincial circuits, occasionally extending their tours to include the major cities. On one such occasion in 1926 in Asakusa, however, a male volunteer was allowed to participate, and women's sumo was once again outlawed in Tokyo, this time for good.

Near the end of the Edo period, beggars put on one-man sumo matches for coins from passers-by. One description of such an exhibition around 1850 reported a performance near the approach to the Ryogoku Bridge near the Eko-in, where pedestrian traffic was heaviest.

A man of about forty years of age, fat, tall, and of heroic complexion, held a towel and a fan in his hands. His clothes were untied, hanging loosely from his body, and he was barefooted. Standing on the side of the road at his customary place, he began to call out in a loud voice, with his fan opened wide, "East—Arauma! . . . West—Koyanagi!"

Immediately men and children began to gather in a crowd around him, realizing that one-man sumo was about to start. As he began to imitate the referee and repeated the names of the wrestlers, some of the spectators yelled out the names of Arauma, and others, Koyanagi. Both sides threw coins in as they called out the name of their favorite. The man climbed onto the ring, "drinking" water and blowing his nose in a funny way, and mimicked the characteristic gestures of the real wrestlers, causing the spectators to laugh. Then he imitated the Kimura and Shikimori referees, saying, "Hakkeyoi!" and then imitated the shikiri and got up again to drink more water. He was extremely close to the real thing.

When the right moment came, he stood up with a yell and began to slap the air. He grappled, pulled apart, and grappled again, and it didn't look like he was alone: it was as if two wrestlers were in front of the crowd. The spectators were tense, and some called out again, "Arauma," while others cheered, "Koyanagi." The two were in a firm clinch and sounded like they were out of breath.

Suddenly the man raised his hands up and looked at the spectators, and said: "Now throw in more coins. If Arauma gets the most, then I'll let him win. If Koyanagi gets the most, then he'll win. Why don't you throw in some money?" The spectators started to throw in more coins, yelling out the wrestlers' names. The clinch wasn't resumed until the coins ceased to fall. Finally the side that threw the most coins won, and the other was dealt a terrible defeat. The spectators all laughed uproariously. If both sides had thrown an equal amount of money, though, it would have been a draw.[8]

End of an Era   The last years of Tokugawa rule, from 1853 to its collapse in 1868, are known as the *bakumatsu,* or the end of the shogunate. This was a period that witnessed the rapid erosion of the authority of the Edo central government and ended in the civil warfare surrounding the restoration of the emperor to power. Sumo, sharing in the uncertainty of the late Edo period, operated at a low key. Anecdotes concerning sumo wrestlers were numerous, however, and closely tied up with the major events of the time.

One of the most important of these exploits was the participation of a group of *miya-zumo* (Shinto-shrine sumo) wrestlers in the decisive seizure of Shimonoseki during the Choshu Civil War of 1865. The feudal domain of Choshu had begun to form a militia composed of both commoners and samurai in 1863, and among these was a troop of wrestlers called the Rikishi Tai (Wrestler-Soldiers). Following Choshu's abortive attack on Kyoto in the summer of 1864, the conservative opponents of the reformist factions in Choshu came back into power and bowed to the demands of the shogunate. Amidst this crisis, the reformist faction managed to gather together some sixty men from the Rikishi Tai, as well as twenty other guerrilla troops.

Even before the Choshu conservatives capitulated to the shogunate, the young samurai, aided by the wrestlers, started armed resistance against the Tokugawa with the blessings of a handful of extremist court nobles who had fled to Choshu. The Rikishi Tai and the guerrillas advanced through the late winter snow in the dead of night toward Shimonoseki to trigger a turning point in the civil war. The ensuing success of the reformist faction led to a strengthening and unifying of the domain that was to enable Choshu to defeat the Tokugawa armies dispatched to subdue it in 1866. Subsequently an alliance between Choshu and the domain of Satsuma was formed, and this eventually resulted in the restoration of 1868. One of the catalysts for restoration had been the attack in which the wrestlers had participated, and later stories of that event had these giants wielding oak timbers, these weapons being better suited to them than swords, for which they had no great skill.

Although it suffered under the events that led to the collapse of the Tokugawa regime, sumo had by the nineteenth century become a popular pastime throughout Japan. Wrestlers were national idols, and the government recognized the importance of sumo. But it was not until Japan entered its modern period that sumo became recognized as the national sport of the country.

4. National Sport of Japan

The Crisis of the Meiji Era During the first few chaotic years of the Meiji era, Edo—made the capital and renamed Tokyo in 1868—had matters far more pressing to attend to than sumo. Even so, in March 1869, when the Meiji Emperor made his historic trip along the Tokaido highway to the new imperial residence at Edo Castle, wrestlers were chosen to walk in front of the procession and bear the imperial banners, the government thus publicly acknowledging their important part in the recent civil warfare. Kyoto wrestlers carried these as far as Shinagawa, on the outskirts of Tokyo, where the banners were then surrendered to the wrestlers from the new capital. In addition, two Tokyo wrestlers participated in the first military review of the newly formed Japanese Army as flag bearers in May the following year, while in June 1869, when construction was begun on Yasukuni Shrine in Tokyo, a number of wrestlers were employed to transport the heavy tree trunks to be used as the nine foundation columns.

As the political renovations of the Meiji Restoration were put into effect, however, enthusiasm and support for sumo itself bottomed out with a resounding thud. For centuries wrestlers had been retained by the great daimyo lords, but with the abolishment of the feudal domains and the assumption of the land registrars by the emperor in 1869, the authority and hereditary incomes of the dai-myo were wiped out in a single stroke, giving most lords no other choice but to immediately release their vassals from service. Samurai were suddenly deprived of their stipends, and wrestlers, who had depended on incomes from the lords, had to find a means of ad-justing to their new economic independence at a time when su-mo's popularity was at an ebb.

The abrupt cutting off of the influence of the daimyo came as a shock to the sumo world, which had already begun to suffer from public censure. As new Western ideas were introduced and adopted almost indiscriminately, succeeding waves of "civilization and enlightenment" swept Japan. In the higher social circles, traditional dress was discarded in favor of the latest London fashions, and a show of modernization was executed with all possible haste. The growing strength of the civilization movement condemned sumo as being unworthy of the modern age. Treatises urging the aboli-tion of sumo began to appear in newspapers, and phrases such as "barbarous sumo should be prohibited" and "the nakedness of sumo is embarrassing" seemed to be the consensus of the day. Fortunately, at the same time that the prevailing sentiment in favor of all things Western led many to call for the abolition of sumo and other aspects of Japanese culture, equally powerful groups in the top echelons of the government supported retention of the country's indigenous traditions. When an edict ordering the bobbing of hair and prohibiting the wearing of swords (the Sampatsu Datto Rei) was enforced in 1871, the topknot of the sumo wrestler was per-mitted to remain untouched through the intervention of a govern-ment magistrate.

Attendance at the biannual tournaments at the Eko-in was poor, however, and continued to decline. The yokozuna Jimmaku re-tired soon after his promotion in 1867 during the confusion of civil warfare. Kimenzan Tanigoro was licensed as yokozuna by the Yoshida officials in March 1869, but, being forty-three years old, he was already well past his prime. He lost two of nine matches during his first tournament as a yokozuna and retired in 1870 with-out completing another. Sakaigawa Namiemon, lauded as "the Tanikaze of the Meiji era," became ozeki that same year and dominated the tournaments until his retirement in 1881. He was awarded yokozuna status in 1876.

What most hindered the Tokyo sumo world in recovering from the crises of the early Meiji era was the autocratic organization of the sumo association. The association, inherited from the Edo period and comprised of select retired wrestlers with the title of

33. *Shiranui Koemon (left), the eleventh yokozuna, and Kimenzan Tanigoro (right), the thirteenth yokozuna, performing the ring-entering ceremony in the 1860s.*

elders, was completely dominated by the *fudegashira,* or director, and the *fudewake,* his assistant. The promotions and demotions of the wrestlers were in the hands of these two, and more often than not their personal prejudices had a great deal to do with determining the ranking lists. Profits from the performances went first to these officials, who then distributed portions to the lesser elders to divide among themselves and their disciples. Little ever made its way to the latter. The system had barely been tolerable during the Edo period, when most of the higher-ranking wrestlers were financially sponsored by the provincial lords, while wrestlers who were not so fortunate generally lived from hand to mouth on irregular and unpredictable earnings, much of which was received from admirers. After the Meiji reforms cut off most sources of outside pay, it became obvious to all but the elders that major changes were needed if sumo was to survive the social crises of the era.

Reform and Resurgence At length an impetuous wrestler named Takamiyama, frustrated by the lack of positive action on the part of the sumo elders in Tokyo, came to the fore and pressed for reforms in the corrupt handling of the finances of the sumo association. Takamiyama joined Edo sumo in 1859 at the age of twenty-one. Upon the recommendation of an influential moneylender, Takamiyama and a number of other wrestlers were employed by Lord Sakai of Himeji around 1865, and a year later he was promoted to juryo rank. At the time of the Meiji Restoration, Takamiyama was deeply involved in a reform movement aimed at the sumo association and demanding better treatment of lower-ranking wrestlers. The momentum of the movement was lost in the confusion then sweeping Japan, and he and the other wrestlers retained by the Himeji clan were dismissed from service because of a lack of funds to pay them. But all immediately vowed that they would maintain their bonds of loyalty to their former master. In 1870, however, one of these wrestlers was approached by the former daimyo of Tosa with an offer of paid employment, and he accepted the position, soon after changing his name to Ayasegawa. Takamiyama was incensed at the defection and attacked Ayasegawa's residence, sword in hand, with the sworn intention of cutting off the traitor's head. The incident was peacefully resolved, however, and eventually the Tokyo elders managed to obtain a written apology from Ayasegawa that settled the matter. Ayasegawa's record was excellent—in 1872 he was promoted to the rank of ozeki—and he and Takamiyama once again became good friends. Takamiyama himself called at the Himeji clan mansion in 1871 to request permission to quit the former daimyo's service. When he parted from the lord, he left with a new name: Takasago Uragoro, after Takasagonoura, a famous beach in Himeji.

In 1873 Takasago, now a maegashira wrestler, and nearly forty other high-ranking wrestlers revived the discarded reform movement. They had all gathered in Nagoya for a joint tournament between Tokyo, Osaka, and that city, when the matches were suddenly postponed, and Takasago took the opportunity to draw up formal amendments to present to the Tokyo elders, touching on the shady financial dealings and arbitrary conduct of the directors. The wrestlers delegated to return to Tokyo with the demands lost their courage, however, and exposed the conspirators to the elders. As the belated Nagoya tournament, set for December, approached, the official ranking lists arrived in the city with the names of Takasago and the other would-be rebels who had stayed behind in Nagoya crossed out. Expelled from the Tokyo sumo association, these outcasts promptly formed their own wrestling group, and, with wrestlers drafted from Osaka and Kyoto, including the future yokozuna Nishinoumi, the "reform wrestling team" performed in the western cities and toured the provinces. In 1876 they returned to

34. *Takasago and his group of wrestlers after returning to Tokyo following their revolt from the sumo association.*

Tokyo to establish a headquarters in Kanda, and for a short time there were two different professional sumo organizations in the capital. In early 1878 the Tokyo metropolitan police issued regulations requiring wrestlers to obtain licenses in order to perform, and Takasago, on tour with over a hundred wrestlers at the time, returned to the capital too late to meet the deadline. After a few uneasy months of negotiation, the two Tokyo teams came to an agreement, and the summer matches that year saw Takasago reinstated in the main sumo body and a series of reforms in its management carried out.

Under these, following each tournament the director and vice-director of the association, together with two ozeki (one each from the eastern and the western teams), would examine the results of the matches and determine the increases and decreases in the post-tournament pay of individual wrestlers accordingly. In addition, it was decided that directors of the association would be selected by election, with the votes of the lower-ranking wrestlers being delegated by the masters of their training stables. Takasago was elected director in 1883. Three years later rules establishing strict relationships between stablemasters and wrestlers were developed. In 1889 the term sumo kaisho was replaced by the name Tokyo Ozumo

Kyokai (Tokyo Grand Sumo Association), and the responsibilities of referees were clearly set down, with the authority over the final judgment of matches transferred from the referee to the judges. Salaries were also revised following the tournaments: after each performance a wrestler's pay would increase in accordance with the number of matches he won, and salaries could be raised accumulatively by tournament until a ceiling of sixty-five yen was reached.

The popular attitude toward sumo, however, still remained one of scorn, although the open support of high-level government leaders such as Saigo Takamori, Ito Hirobumi, and Kuroda Kiyotaka kept the more impetuous advocates of the "enlightenment" movement from abolishing sumo altogether. The wrestlers themselves were well aware of the need for action to bring about a shift in public opinion. In 1876, in response to a suggestion from Saigo and others, a group of them volunteered to form a separate battalion of the Tokyo Metropolitan Fire Brigade. During the civil uprisings that occurred in the late 1870s, too, wrestlers were publically lauded for their service to the emperor. Even so, the situation remained uncertain for some time. In 1882, for example, a complaint was filed with the Tokyo police that the sound of the scaffold drum that had been erected near the tournament grounds was too loud, and the deputy chief of police simply ordered sumo prohibited. The sumo association was stunned, but through a petition endorsed by Ito Hirobumi, the prohibition was overruled.

The reckless rush to westernize the country eventually produced an inevitable popular counterreaction aimed at preventing the disappearance of Japan's traditional culture, and when in early 1884 the emperor Meiji ordered sumo performed before him to emphasize his support of it, a definite change in attitude could be detected. Enthusiasm for sumo arose in all quarters. With the appearance soon thereafter of the champion wrestlers Umegatani, Odate, and Nishinoumi, sumo quickly began to recover.

Late-Nineteenth-Century Champions   Umegatani Totaro I was born in 1845 in Fukuoka Prefecture, the son of a papermaker. At the age of seventeen he joined the Minato stable of Osaka and adopted as his professional wrestling name that of his home village, Umegatani. By 1870 he had advanced through the ranks of Osaka sumo to the position of ozeki, but that winter he left for Tokyo, where he apprenticed himself to the elder Tamagaki. The contemptuous attitude of Tokyo wrestlers toward their Osaka counterparts forced Umegatani to the bottom of the ranking list, and although his performance

35. Wrestlers wielding staves and logs during the civil uprising of 1877.

in the tournaments was excellent, the prejudice of the directors made his advancement slow. In 1874 Umegatani was at length admitted to the makuuchi division, but although he had few rivals, it was 1879 before he was advanced to ozeki rank. There he remained for six years. Finally, just prior to the imperial tournament of 1884, Umegatani was licensed as yokozuna by both the Gojo and the Yoshida families. In early 1885, during his second tournament as yokozuna, he was beaten two days in a row, however, and thereupon retired. He adopted the name Ikazuchi Gondaiyu as an elder and became one of the foremost leaders of the sumo association for two full decades. In 1915, when his favorite disciple, the yokozuna Umegatani Totaro II, retired, Gondaiyu passed on to him his elder name and left the sumo world entirely, although he continued to be called Oikazuchi (Great Ikazuchi) until his death at the age of eighty-three.

Odate Hane-emon was one of the most powerful of all the early Meiji-era wrestlers, although he was never promoted to yokozuna status. Born in 1856 in Yamagata Prefecture, he entered Tokyo sumo as a disciple of the elder Asahidake. He joined the rebellious Takasago as a member of the reform team, returning to Tokyo sumo in 1878 as a makushita wrestler. Odate was only a komusubi

36. *Odate and Tsurugiyama, both of whom were promoted to ozeki status in late 1885, performing before the Meiji emperor.*

when in late 1884 he beat the hitherto unrivaled Umegatani, after having wrestled him to a draw in front of the emperor the previous March. The following year his master, Takasago, promoted stablemate Nishinoumi to ozeki status, skipping over Odate in spite of the fact that the latter's record was better. After quarreling with Takasago about this, Odate was expelled from the stable. Deploring Taksasago's highhanded dealings, the elder Isenoumi took Odate under his protection, and in early 1888 the wrestler was finally promoted to ozeki status. Odate was already forty-two years old, and two years later he retired to become an elder himself.

Nishinoumi Kajiro I, from Kagoshima Prefecture, joined Kyoto sumo in 1875 at the age of twenty but quit to become a member of Takasago's reform team in Nagoya soon afterward. He made his debut in Tokyo in early 1882 as a makuuchi wrestler under Takasago's influence and was raised briefly to ozeki status in 1885. Nishinoumi regained that rank in 1890 and was promoted to yokozuna status in the next tournament. After he complained that his name was to be listed on an outcropping to one side of the program as a *haridashi* ozeki, Takasago ordered that the word "yokozuna" be added next to Nishinoumi's name to placate the champion, the first time that the characters ever appeared on a program.

With his rise to power in the sumo association, Takasago seems to have forgotten his own former anger at the unfairness of that body, and he soon began to abuse his position. Dissatisfaction with his highhanded ways and his increasing favoritism toward his own disciples led to a general rebellion against the director. Tempers began to reach the breaking point in the summer of 1895. On the sixth day of the tournament being held at that time, the yokozuna Nishinoumi was called by the referee as having stepped out of bounds, and his opponent, the maegashira Ho-o (who became ozeki in 1897), was declared the winner. The wrestlers on Nishinoumi's side complained, and the judges could not reach a verdict. Finally Takasago himself mounted the ring. Walking over to the side, he stated that there was a heel print only on the top of the straw bale at the edge, not on the outside, and, erasing an obvious footprint that was embedded in the sand beyond the boundary of the ring, declared the referee had been mistaken. The judges were shocked at his action, and most of them would not accept the decision. Discussions continued well into the night, with the spectators losing patience and returning home. The match was finally called a draw, but Nishinoumi declined to appear the following day and retired as yokozuna after the next tournament. Calling himself Izutsu, he revived the old stable of that name and served as its stablemaster until his death at the age of fifty-three.

In January of the following year Takasago attempted to place another of his disciples, Konishiki, on the same side as Ho-o— that of the western team—in order to avoid any possibility of Konishiki losing to Ho-o in a match. Affronted, the wrestlers of Ho-o's team protested by not appearing at the matches, several of them leaving Tokyo to join Osaka sumo. Even the wrestlers of the eastern team, of which Takasago's disciples were members, resented the director's undisguised favoritism and joined in submitting an ultimatum for explicit reforms to the directors of the sumo association. As a result, the rules of the association underwent revision in February, and Takasago retired after sharing the position of director for two more tournaments with the elder Ikazuchi (the former Umegatani I). With Takasago gone, Ikazuchi took up sole leadership of the Tokyo sumo world.

Champion wrestlers, having earlier lost nearly all of the powerful daimyo sponsors, began to be supported by wealthy patron organizations in the middle of the Meiji era. Two of the earliest of these were the Hinoshita Kai (Champion Club) and the Banzai Kai (Ten Thousand Year Club). The latter, which began to present decorated aprons to undefeated wrestlers, was not originally

37. *The practice quarters for the eastern team in the early Meiji era.*

associated with any particular stable. After Araiwa, who was ozeki between 1905 and 1909, was twice given aprons by the group, the Ten Thousand Year Club gradually became the patron of the Oguruma stable, to which Araiwa belonged, and changed its name to the Oguruma Club. Another organization, called the Dokan Kai (Empathy Club), also developed to support Hitachiyama, who became yokozuna in 1903. Journals specializing in sumo also began to appear. A short-lived newspaper called the *Rikishi shimpo* (Wrestlers' Report) emerged briefly in 1889. In 1897 *Sumo shimpo* (Sumo Report) was first printed, and it was followed by *Sumo shimbun* (Sumo News) seven years later.

Hitachiyama and Umegatani II   In 1903 Hitachiyama Taniemon and Umegatani Totaro II were promoted to yokozuna status. With the sudden period of national prosperity and the surge of nationalistic fervor that swept Japan following the country's exhilarating victory over Russia in 1905, the rivalry between "Hitachi" and "Ume" spurred on the building of widespread popular support for sumo.

Hitachiyama Taniemon will always remain one of the most famous names in modern sumo history. He was born in 1874, the eldest son of a family of swordsmen named Ichige of Ibaraki

Prefecture. The bankruptcy of his father led the family to move to Tokyo, where the boy entered junior high school. A former disciple of his father's who happened to be employed at the school as a *kendo* (swordsmanship) instructor noted the boy's strength and introduced him to the master of the Dewanoumi stable, the former Hitachiyama Torakichi. Proud of their samurai heritage, Hitachiyama's father and grandfather at first opposed the idea of the boy becoming a wrestler, but at length, in 1891, the boy entered the Dewanoumi stable as an apprentice. Three years later he inherited the name Hitachiyama. In 1895 he left Tokyo with the ozeki Oikari to perform in Nagoya and Osaka, joining the Nakamura stable in Osaka the following year. There Hitachiyama stayed until he rejoined Tokyo sumo in May 1897 as a makushita wrestler: less than two years later he stood at the top of that rank. At that time he weighed less than two hundred and fifty pounds, but before the end of his career he added another seventy-five pounds to his bulk. In 1901 he was advanced to ozeki rank. Four years after his promotion to yokozuna status following the summer tournament of 1903, Hitachiyama and three of his disciples traveled to the United States, where he was presented to the president, Theodore Roosevelt. They met in the reception hall of the executive offices

38.   *Hitachiyama, who became the nineteenth yokozuna in 1903, performing the ring-entering ceremony.*

入 俵 土 綱 横 山 陸 常

of the White House, where the Americans saw for the first time an elaborate presentation of the Japanese ceremonial bow. "Hitachi-yama doubled himself up," reported the *New York Times,* "with a sibilant inspiration that sounded like escaping steam whistling through a cracked pipe. It was a proud performance for one of his embonpoint, but long practice had rendered him almost graceful at it, and he astonished the spectators at the way he got through with it."[1] After accepting a priceless old sword from the wrestler, a blade that had been given to Hitachiyama by his former feudal clan when he was awarded yokozuna status, the president made arrangements to see the Japanese wrestlers in the group perform after he returned from a hunting trip in Louisiana. A month later the wrestler and his disciples gave a small exhibition of their prowess on the tennis courts behind the White House. The following day's newspapers noted that the president, the ambassador from India, and members of the cabinet "sat in a row along one side of the ring when they were not so excited by the performance that they hopped about like football enthusiasts on the side lines at a big game."[2]

After touring Europe, Hitachiyama returned to Japan in 1908. Retiring in 1914, he inherited the name and elder status of his stablemaster, Dewanoumi, and remained a major figure in the Grand Sumo Association until his death in 1922. Three of his disciples—Onishiki, Tochigiyama, and Tsunenohana—became yokozuna, and many others reached the higher ranks of the makuuchi division, establishing the Dewanoumi stable as a producer of champion wrestlers.

Umegatani Totaro II, born the son of a druggist in 1878 in To-yama Prefecture, was considered the "master wrestler," a champion with total control of the techniques requiring delicate timing and maneuvering. He was discovered in 1891 by the ozeki Tsurugiyama, whose master, Ikazuchi (the former Umegatani I), invited the boy to join his stable. By early 1898, after his promotion to the makuuchi division, the young wrestler was recognized as Hitachiyama's primary rival. Umenotani (he inherited his master's full wrestling name when he became yokozuna) was advanced to ozeki status two years later and was promoted to yokozuna rank in 1903 with Hitachiyama. The rivalry between the two yokozuna lasted over a decade. In May 1915, one year after Hitachiyama's retirement, Umegatani left the ring himself and inherited the elder name Ikazuchi from his former master. He and Dewanoumi (Hitachiyama) led the sumo association for years; the death of "Hitachi" in 1922 and of "Ume" in 1929 marked the end of an era in the sumo world.

At the same time that the "Hitachi-Ume" duo was thrilling au-

39. Hitachiyama (left) and Umegatani posing. The referee is the
twenty-third generation Yoshida
Oikaze.

diences in Tokyo, a wrestler by the name of Wakashima Gonshiro
was gaining attention in Osaka. Born in 1876 in Chiba Prefecture,
Wakashima joined Tokyo's Tachiyama stable at the age of fifteen.
By early 1896 he was wrestling in the makuuchi division, but while
on tour two years later he quit Tokyo sumo to join the Nakamura
stable in Osaka. He was promoted to ozeki there in 1902 and in
early 1903 received permission from the Gojo family to perform the
duties of yokozuna. Two years later his advancement was ratified
by the Yoshida family. Wakashima was popular in great part for
his handsome Western-type features, but his fame as a champion
wrestler was well justified. When Osaka and Tokyo wrestlers met
for combined tournaments, Hitachiyama was his only real challenger. An injury incurred while on tour in late 1905 led to his
retirement from sumo two years later, however, and he left the sumo
world entirely, dying at the age of sixty-eight in 1943.

National Stadium In 1909 the first Kokugikan, the national sumo
stadium, was constructed in the Ryogoku district of Tokyo, just to
one side of the Eko-in temple precincts. The stadium was designed by
Tatsuno Kingo, who also drew up the plans for the Tokyo Railway
Station. A number of suggestions were made for the name of the

new building, but when a reporter casually dropped the phrase *kokugi* (national sport) in a newspaper article announcing the completion of the hall, the sumo association decided that the term was perfect for the building that was to be the home of sumo; *kan* indicates a stadium or hall.

That year the association also supplemented its regulations so that henceforth makuuchi wrestlers would perform on all ten days of the tournaments, instead of only nine, as was customary throughout the Edo period. The costume of the referees, which had previously been the traditional ceremonial garb of the samurai, was changed to informal warrior's kimono and black court hats.

Beginning with the opening of the stadium in 1909, a championship banner was awarded to the winning team on the final day of the tournament. In addition, the Jiji Shimpo-sha (later absorbed by the Mainichi Press) began to present the champion wrestler of each tournament with a framed portrait that was to be hung in the stadium. With the completion of the new building, the general character of the audience began to change, and the "undignified" practice of allowing individuals in the audience to throw articles of clothing and money into the wrestling ring, as well as the wandering of peddlers about the theater, was prohibited.

Built with a seating capacity of 13,000, the new building, however, did not always attract capacity audiences, and the financial reserves of the Grand Sumo Association were sorely depleted after paying for the construction of the hall. When in 1911 the lower-ranking wrestlers led a mass strike for increased pay, the sumo elders faced grave difficulties. Fortunately a compromise was reached through outside mediation, although neither side was completely satisfied with the settlement, in which it was decided that the final financial accounting of the association would be overseen by representatives chosen from among the high-ranking wrestlers, and that ten percent of the total income from each tournament would be paid as bonuses to all wrestlers but yokozuna and ozeki. Two-thirds of that ten percent would be received as a cash payment, with the remaining one-third being placed in a pension fund.

Meanwhile in Kyoto, sumo, which never recovered from the blows dealt to it by the Restoration, was at its lowest level of popularity in history. In an attempt to buttress the fallen prestige of the city's wrestlers, thirty-five of them, under the leadership of the Kyoto yokozuna Oikari Taro, accepted an invitation to perform for the opening of a Japanese exhibition hall in London to commemorate the signing of the Anglo-Japanese Alliance. They left from Yokohama in 1910 and spent four and a half months performing in England. After the exhibit closed, Oikari and the other wrestlers went to Paris to begin an extended European tour. Halfway through, a number of wrestlers headed for home, but Oikari and the rest continued to ply their trade in foreign realms, crossing to South America in 1913. After returning once more to Europe, they finally headed for Japan, arriving after an absence of three and a half years. Oikari, however, had stayed behind in Argentina. Tragically, he lost the job he had found there and spent his final days toiling in coolie labor. Back in Kyoto, with the combination of the prolonged absence of the major wrestlers and the emigration of the star yokozuna, sumo lost what support it had had left, eventually dying there from lack of interest.

In Tokyo, as Hitachiyama and Umegatani passed their primes, great new wrestlers came forward. Tachiyama Mine-emon, born in 1877 in Toyama Prefecture to a peasant family, became the twenty-second yokozuna in 1911. He was discovered at the age of twenty-one by the elder Tomozuna, and, because of his great strength and size—he stood almost six feet two inches in height—he was placed in the makushita division in his first professional tournament in the summer of 1900. Three years later he was advanced to the makuuchi division and in 1905 was promoted to sekiwake rank. He was given the rank of ozeki in the summer of 1909 at the opening of the Kokugikan and became yokozuna two years later. Tachiyama's style was likened to that of the famed Edo-period star Raiden. After the retirements of Hitachiyama and Umegatani, Tachiyama became the star of Tokyo sumo. He won eleven championships, five of them with no losses, and at one time won fifty-six matches in succession. He retired in 1918 and left the sumo world completely at that time.

The Kokugikan was destroyed by fire in 1917, and, until its reconstruction two years later, annual tournaments were held in the precincts of the Yasukuni Shrine. Onishiki Uichiro became yokozuna in 1917 and was followed by Tochigiyama Moriya the next year. Onishiki, known in his day as "the founder of modern sumo," was born in 1891 in the city of Osaka. He was remarkably well educated for a wrestler, having almost finished junior high school when he joined the Dewanoumi stable in Tokyo. Eight tournaments later saw him advanced to the juryo division, and following an undefeated championship in the summer of 1914 he was promoted to makuuchi status. He advanced to ozeki rank in record time, defeated the champion Tachiyama in early 1917, and was awarded yokozuna status that year. In 1923, at the peak of his career, he assumed responsibility for a general strike among the wrestlers—

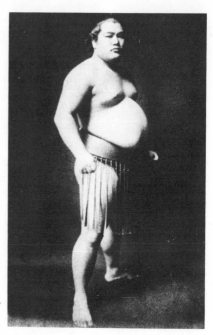

40. *Onishiki Daigoro displaying his girth for the camera in the early 1920s.*

known as the Mikawajima incident—and retired from the sumo world. He later continued his studies and eventually became a reporter for the *Howa shimbun*.

By and large the biannual Tokyo tournaments failed to attract great crowds in the late 1910s, and debts incurred in rebuilding the Kokugikan in 1919 further depleted the resources of the Grand Sumo Association. In 1923 yet another strike by wrestlers occurred. When mediation by the yokozuna Onishiki failed to satisfy their demands, the strikers locked themselves up in an electrical factory in Mikawajima. The head of the metropolitan police stepped in, and finally an agreement, which allowed for a fifty-percent increase in wrestlers' pensions, was reached. To finance this further drain on the association's reserves, the length of the tournaments was extended from ten to eleven days. Onishiki, who caused a major scandal by involving the police in the incident, cut off his topknot, supposedly done of his own accord, and left the sumo world, although it was rumored that he was forced to retire because of complicated conflicting interests within the association in regard to a successor to the director Dewanoumi (the former Hitachiyama), who had died the previous year.

Hardly had the incident subsided when the Kokugikan was completely burned down again during the Great Kanto Earthquake of September 1923, which reduced the greater part of Tokyo to rubble. The spring tournament of 1924 was held in Nagoya but attracted few spectators. An athletic field was completed in the outer park of the Meiji Shrine in Tokyo that year, and ritual sumo was performed between the eastern and western teams at the opening ceremonies.

National Sumo Association   In late April 1925, the prince regent (the present Emperor Hirohito) invited the Tokyo Sumo Association to perform at the Togu Palace. Afterwards, a large sum of money was given the association by the Ministry of the Imperial Household to establish a trophy for the champion individual wrestler, with the suggestion that Osaka wrestlers also be eligible. The question of a possible merger of the Tokyo and Osaka sumo associations had been brought up in the early 1920s, but an agreement was never reached between the two. During the Edo period there were sumo organizations in Nagoya and Kyoto, but they went into decline after the Meiji Restoration until they were little more than amateur groups. In Osaka, however, professional wrestlers had continued to perform regularly. Internal strife in the Osaka sumo organization and the group's contacts with gamblers and ruffians lent to it a rather sordid character, but even so, Osaka yokozuna were still appointed and ratified by the Yoshida officials.

In spite of its tenacity, however, even wrestling in Osaka had been on the decline since the beginning of World War I. Thus when the Tokyo sumo association extended an invitation to join forces in 1925, the response was a warm one. Formal consolidation took place soon afterwards in Osaka. To compile the combined lists of ranking, qualifying tournaments were held in November 1925 and in March and October of the following year. The Osaka yokozuna Miyagiyama retained his position, although few other Osaka wrestlers managed to stay in the top ranks. Miyagiyama won the championship at the first joint sumo tournament in 1927 but retired in early 1931, adopting the elder name Shibatayama. The Osaka elder Minato (formerly the yokozuna Okido Moriemon) left the sumo world entirely upon the amalgamation of the two teams. Both Miyagiyama and Okido, the last of the Osaka yokozuna, died in 1943.

With the joining together of the Tokyo and Osaka sumo associations, the All-Japan Grand Sumo Association (Dai Nihon Ozumo Kyokai) was born. In ensuing years this organization was to change its name several times before finally settling on the Japan Sumo Association (Nihon Sumo Kyokai) in 1958. It was formally instituted as a nonprofit organization in 1927, and, because in Japan all nonprofit corporations are required to be registered with a government office, sumo was put under the auspices of the Ministry of Education. Legally, the association's primary purpose was to train wrestlers, and it was expected that it would establish a special school, but this was not actually done until 1957.

When live radio broadcasting of the tournaments began in 1928, strict time limits were for the first time placed on the warm-up delays of the wrestlers. These were set at ten minutes for those of makuuchi rank, seven minutes for those of juryo rank, and five minutes for makushita wrestlers and those of lower status. At first the officials of the sumo association, with the sole exception of the director, Dewanoumi (the former ozeki Ryogoku Kajinosuke, a disciple of Hitachiyama), were opposed to the broadcasting. Dewanoumi had the foresight to realize that through radio sumo would become more popular, rather than lose spectators, as the others feared. He was right, and the audiences began to swell.

In response to the demands of spectators, the four judges, who had sat with their backs against the four pillars of the ring since the middle of the Edo period, moved in 1930 to below the wrestling platform so that their huge bodies did not obstruct the view of the audience. Imperial viewings of sumo took place at the palace in Tokyo in 1930 and 1931, adding the highest sanction to the sport.

Sumo was once more on the upswing, recovering from the depression of the early 1920s and competing favorably with the appeal of the more modern sport of baseball, when in January 1932 most of the high-ranking wrestlers deserted the sumo association in what was known as the Shunju-en Incident. In this, all of the makuuchi wrestlers of the Dewanoumi stable, led by the sekiwake Tenryu Saburo, locked themselves up in the Shunju-en, a Chinese restaurant in Tokyo, after submitting a demand to the association's officials for both a clear definition of the wrestlers' rights and better treatment in the stables. Although the ozeki Musashiyama had second thoughts about participating and returned to the Dewanoumi stable, a total of twenty makuuchi and eleven juryo wrestlers of the western team joined Tenryu in revolt. Major-General Kido of the army and other prominent military officers offered to act as mediators in the incident, but the rebellious wrestlers rejected these attempts at conciliation. Cutting their hair short, the dissidents formed a new team, completely severing their ties with the association. Seventeen high-ranking wrestlers of the eastern team then also left the association and formed the Revolutionary Wres-

41. *Announcers parading the streets and beating drums to give notice of the opening of the 1937 tournament.*

tling Team, and the two new groups traveled through the provinces, giving performances.

With over half of the makuuchi and juryo wrestlers gone, the sumo elders were forced to promote lower-ranking wrestlers one after another to fill the empty positions. Futabayama Sadaji, who later became one of sumo's greatest champions, advanced from the rank of juryo to that of an upper maegashira. In the meantime, the new wrestling groups gained in popularity for a while but soon began to lose their audiences. Tamanishiki San'emon was promoted to yokozuna in July 1932 and Musashiyama Takeshi in July 1935. As the Tokyo wrestlers regained their popularity and the reformed wrestling groups lost theirs, one after another the deserters returned to the capital. Asashio, who had been deprived of that name when he joined the defectors, was reinstated as Minanogawa Tozo and was magnanimously allowed to become a yokozuna in 1936, three years following his return.

The true star of the late 1930s and early 1940s, however, was Futabayama. This wrestler, a legend in his own time, was born in 1912 in Oita Prefecture, the son of a boatman. For years after he joined the Tatsunami stable in 1927 there seemed to be nothing

42. *Tamanishiki performing the ring-entering ceremony at the Kokugikan. Circa 1930.*

43. *The fabulous Futabayama in the midst of his ring-entering ceremony after being made yokozuna in 1937.*

special about the wrestler, but following his abrupt promotion to makuuchi status in 1932, Futabayama began to prove his worth. With his advancement to the sekiwake position in 1936, he suddenly gained weight, and his wrestling style changed dramatically. He started on a long winning streak after gaining the January 1936 tournament title and remained undefeated until he lost to a maegashira wrestler by the name of Akinoumi in a match that had been expected to be Futabayama's seventieth straight victory. During that period he was promoted first to ozeki in January 1937 and then to yokozuna in the following May. The upsetting of Futabayama caused a furor in Tokyo, and newspapers issued extras just to announce the shocking news. Losing only one other championship (in 1940), Futabayama continued to have few rivals, although Haguroyama Masaji, Akinoumi Setsuo, and Terukuni Manzo were promoted to yokozuna status in 1941 and 1942. Before announcing his retirement in the fall of 1945, Futabayama won twelve championships, eight of which were undefeated.

An enormous surge in sumo's popularity led the association to extend the tournaments to thirteen days in May 1937 and to fifteen days in early 1940. The east-west competition, which had been replaced by competition between stables after the Shunju-en incident, was restored in 1940. The warm-up time was further shortened in 1942 to seven minutes for makuuchi wrestlers, five minutes for juryo wrestlers, and four minutes for the wrestlers of the lower ranks.

With the escalation of the war with China in the late 1930s and the opening of the Pacific War in December 1941, the phrase "the undefeated Imperial Army" became common parlance, and Futabayama's performance appeared to all to be a symbol of the times. Sumo was included as a required subject in the physical-education programs of the elementary schools. As baseball and other sports of foreign origin were widely denounced, sumo rode high in public favor, and professional wrestlers crossed the waters to perform for the Imperial Army in the occupied areas of China and Manchuria. In the summer of 1942, however, the war began to turn against the Japanese. Most of the younger wrestlers were drafted and departed for the front, while those left behind were formed into physical-labor units by stable to work in the provinces. The Kokugikan was requisitioned by the military forces in 1944, and the summer and winter tournaments of that year took place on the baseball diamond at the Koraku-en park. By 1945 the air raids over Tokyo became so severe that the January tournament was called off, and in March, when the stadium and most of the stables

44. *Sumo once again returned to the outdoors in 1944 when the Imperial Army requisitioned the Kokugikan and the tournaments had to be held at Koraku-en park.*

were heavily damaged by fire, a number of wrestlers perished. That summer, matches were performed by upper-ranking wrestlers in the ruins of the Kokugikan, but only members of the sumo association were allowed to attend. Then in August 1945 Japan surrendered to the Allied forces.

Postwar Confusion In November 1945 the sumo association received permission from the Occupation authorities to hold a ten-day tournament in the damaged Kokugikan. For this occasion the wrestling ring was widened to sixteen feet in diameter, but the consensus of wrestlers and audience alike was that it was too large—and seemed even larger, many remarked, because so many wrestlers had shrunk in girth due to the scarcity of food. The traditional fifteen-foot ring was revived the following year. Haguroyama and the newly promoted makuuchi wrestler Chiyonoyama both won all of their matches—it was not yet possible for a lower-ranking makuuchi wrestler to be pitted against a yokozuna—but the championship cup went to Haguroyama, since, by tradition, in the case of a tie the title went to the wrestler who was senior in rank. Immediately after the performance, the Kokugikan was requisitioned by the Occupation forces. Renamed Memorial Hall, it was partially made into a skating rink for American soldiers.

With the Kokugikan lost, the only tournament in 1946 was in November, when the sumo association received special permission to hold a final thirteen-day tournament in the old wrestling stadium. Following this tournament, the great Futabayama officially retired (he had announced his retirement the previous year), performing his final ring-entering ceremony flanked by the yokozuna Terukuni and Haguroyama before an emotional audience.

In 1947, access to the Kokugikan forbidden it, the association obtained permission to use the sumo arena in the Meiji Shrine Outer Gardens for tournaments. Spectators entering the grounds were confronted by volunteers collecting signatures to demand the restoration of the Kokugikan to the wrestlers, but the movement never got very far, and tournaments continued to be held outdoors in the park until 1949, when a temporary stadium built of galvanized iron sheets was set up in Hamacho Park.

In June 1947 Maedayama Eigoro was promoted to the rank of yokozuna to become the first grand champion of the postwar period. Born in 1914 in Ehime prefecture, he joined the Takasago stable at the age of fifteen. He was temporarily expelled from the

45.   Futabayama's topknot being cut at his retirement ceremony in 1946. His record for most successive wins still stands.

stable not long afterwards for fighting, and at one point he dropped from juryo to sandamme status while recovering from a bout with bone disease. After finally reaching the makuuchi division in 1937, he needed only three tournaments to advance to the rank of ozeki. He remained an ozeki for nine and a half years, attacking his opponents Futabayama and Haguroyama with a rough, if not always successful, style of sumo that delighted the audience. He was finally promoted to yokozuna status at the age of thirty-three but retired in September 1949 when he drew criticism for being seen at a baseball game after having withdrawn from a tournament partway through. In spite of his short and unimpressive career as yokozuna—he lost twenty-nine of his fifty-three matches—Maedayama went on to make sizable contributions as an official of the sumo association after retirement. He was also master of the Takasago stable until his death in 1971.

During the summer of 1947 the play-off system (*kettei sen*) was set up. If two wrestlers tied for the championship of a tournament, no longer would the cup automatically go to the senior in rank of the two, but rather a special play-off match would be held between them at the end of the final tournament day. The individual prize system was also instituted, changing the traditional east-west competition to one between all the wrestlers and creating three special awards—fighting spirit (*kanto-sho*), technique (*gino-sho*), and outstanding performer (*shukun-sho*)—for makuuchi wrestlers under the rank of ozeki. In the fall of 1948 a tournament was held in Osaka for the first time since the war, and there the sekiwake Masuiyama won his first championship after an exciting play-off with the winner of the summer tournament, Azumafuji. The latter was promoted to yokozuna and Masuiyama to ozeki following the tournament.

Azumafuji Kin'ichi, a native of Tokyo, was born in 1921. He joined the Fujigane stable in 1929 (later he became a member of the Takasago stable) and began his career in the makuuchi division in 1943 with a flourish, defeating all but one opponent in his first tournament. He was promoted to ozeki status in 1945 and to yokozuna three years later. Holding the record as the all-time heaviest yokozuna at almost three hundred and eighty pounds, Azumafuji ended his career with an uneven record and retired in 1954 after winning six championships during his twelve years as a makuuchi wrestler. He served as an elder for a while but then retired from the sumo world to turn to professional Western-style wrestling. He later acted as a sumo critic for television and sports newspapers. He died in 1973.

46. *Postwar tournament at the makeshift stadium in Hamacho Park, which was used until 1949. American soldiers sit with their backs to the camera.*

In January of 1950 the yokozuna Haguroyama, Azumafuji, and Terukuni all dropped out midway through the tournament. In the ensuing furor, demands arose for their demotion, and succeeding discussions led to the formation of a yokozuna review committee to establish standards for the holders of that status and to recommend wrestlers for promotion to that rank. Its ten members were all distinguished representatives of fields unconnected with the sumo world and included academicians, sociologists, and writers. (Terukuni regained public favor by making a sudden comeback in the fall tournament, downing Yoshibayama in a play-off match to win his first tournament cup.) In January 1951 the sumo association declared that the licensing of yokozuna would be entirely under the jurisdiction of the review committee and the directors of the association, making the traditional recommendation and approval of the Yoshida officials merely ceremonial. The awarding of the championship portraits by the Mainichi Press, suspended during the war, was resumed in May, and Terukuni's likeness became the first to be hung in the new Kokugikan—construction of which was begun in 1950—after he won the March tournament in 1951. Chiyonoyama won the summer tournament, following which he was promoted to yokozuna status.

Chiyonoyama Masanobu, rising to a towering height of six feet two and a half inches, was the first yokozuna to be born in Hokkaido. He joined the Dewanoumi stable in 1942 at the age of sixteen, and during his first tournament as a makuuchi wrestler in November 1945, he won all ten of his matches to tie with the yokozuna Haguroyama. After being promoted to yokozuna status himself in the fall of 1951, Chiyonoyama remained in that rank for eight years. After retirement in 1959, he assumed the name Kokonoe as an elder, and in 1967 he left his position as a coach of the Dewanoumi stable to begin his own stable under the Kokonoe name. He died in 1977.

Tournaments, meanwhile, took place in the unfinished Kokugikan, which by 1952 was beginning to take on an identifiable shape in the Kuramae district of Tokyo. Banners with the names of individual wrestlers, which had been outlawed since the opening of the Ryogoku Kokugikan in 1909, once more fluttered colorfully in the breeze after a forty-three year hiatus. Inside, just prior to the fall 1952 tournament, the four posts surrounding the ring were removed to make viewing easier. These were replaced by four large colored tassels hanging from a roof suspended below the ceiling of the building. Live television broadcasting began the following summer.

In the summer of 1953 Kagamisato Kiyoshi was promoted to yokozuna, with Yoshibayama Junnosuke following him in early 1954.

The construction of the Kokugikan was finally completed in September 1954, at which time a sumo museum was opened in the outer building of the complex. Sumo surged in popularity with the advent of television broadcasting, and at first four different channels competed in airing the tournaments. By the early 1960s the government station, NHK, emerged with a monopoly over sumo. At the same time, with the rivalry between the wrestlers Tochinishiki and Wakanohana, the sport picked up momentum with every tournament.

The Tochi-Waka Era Tochinishiki Kiyotaka, born in Tokyo in 1925, began work in a pulp mill soon after finishing elementary school. He was just thirteen years old when he joined the Kasugano stable. In May 1944 he adopted the name Tochinishiki, using the first character of Tochigiyama, the former wrestling name of his master. Tochinishiki was always small for a wrestler, having barely passed the height and weight requirements for apprenticeship, and he only stood five feet nine inches and weighed one hundred sixty-five pounds at the time of his advancement to the makuuchi division in 1947. He was promoted to ozeki in January 1953 and to yokozuna following the September 1954 tournament.

Wakanohana Kanji, known as the "devil of the ring" (*dohyo*

47. *The Kokugikan in Kuramae while still under construction in the early 1950s, with the drum scaffolding in front. Patrons' offerings of sakè in huge kegs are stacked on each side of the entrance.*

48. *The Kuramae Kokugikan before the four pillars were removed from around the ring. The wrestlers are performing the ring-entering ceremony.*

no oni), was born in 1928 in Aomori Prefecture. After the devastating failure of his father's apple orchards just when the boy had begun elementary school, the family moved to Hokkaido, where the father found work as a longshoreman. A few years later he enlisted in the army, and to support the family the young Wakanohana got work in a coal mine. The labor there shaped his body and toned his muscles, and in the summer of 1946 rumors of his strength reached a group of Nishonoseki-stable wrestlers performing in the area. The youth turned out to be so small in stature that the Nishonoseki stablemaster at first dismissed him as a possible disciple, but after watching him wrestle, he realized that the boy had a natural feel for sumo. That fall Wakanohana, aged seventeen, appeared in his first tournament as a member of the Nishonoseki stable; in 1953 he was transferred to the new Hanakago stable. By early 1950 he had become a makuuchi wrestler, and he was promoted to ozeki rank following the fall tournament of 1955. A year later he was being considered for promotion to yokozuna status, after having won the January tournament, tied in the March tournament, and won the May championship. Just prior to the beginning of the September matches, however, his four-year-old eldest son was fatally scalded by an overturned cooking pot in the Hanakago stable kitchen; Wakanohana attended the tournament in mourning with a wooden Buddhist rosary strung about his neck. He won every match during the first twelve days but then dropped out of the tournament, eliminating any chance he had of being advanced to the yokozuna rank. It was not until February 1958, after the retirement of the yokozuna Yoshibayama and Kagamisato, that he was finally promoted to that status.

The years from the promotion of Tochinishiki to komusubi status and Wakanohana to maegashira until Tochinishiki's retirement in March 1960 were the "Tochi-Waka" era. Both were trim and handsome, and they proved to be great favorites in those early years of television broadcasting. Matches between the two were anticipated with nearly as much fervor as any between Tanikaze and Onogawa or Hitachiyama and Umegatani. Of the thirty-three times they faced each other over nine years, Tochinishiki won eighteen and Wakanohana fifteen. Both won ten tournament cups before their retirements (Wakanohana retired in 1962). Tochinishiki became the master of the Kasugano stable and is presently the chairman of the board of directors of the sumo association, while Wakanohana is the master of the Futagoyama stable.

In 1957 a massive shake-up of the sumo association resulted from an uproar that broke out over the questionable manner in which the theoretically nonprofit income of the organization was being handled. The inner workings of the Japan Sumo Association were examined in a special Diet session instigated by widespread public criticism over the extreme difficulties involved in obtaining box seats at tournaments. The teahouses had long monopolized the sale of blocks of tickets to favored patrons, and during the Diet investigation it was revealed that the wife and daughter of the chairman of the sumo association, Dewanoumi (the former Tsunenohana), ran two of the biggest of these. The manner in which the association was being governed came under such heavy attack that Dewanoumi, faced with scandal, attempted to commit harakiri. He was replaced as chairman by Tokitsukaze (Futaba-yama), under whose leadership, which lasted until his death in 1968, important reforms were made. An agreement was reached whereby forty percent of all tickets would be sold to the general public without recourse to the teahouses, which were renamed ticket and guide offices (*annai-jo*) and grouped under the heading of the Sumo Service Company. A sumo training institute was officially opened in October 1957, and all newly-entering wrestlers were required to spend six months studying subjects that ranged from sumo history and medical treatment for sports injuries to calligraphy and poetry reading. The traditional pay system for wrestlers was changed from a periodic bonus system to monthly wages, establishing salaries for all wrestlers of juryo rank and higher. An independent referee stable was also established, and a fifth annual tournament was added in Fukuoka every November. The sixth and final annual tournament was inaugurated in Nagoya in July 1958. Two years later the referee system was further revised, and from that time it became customary for the referees who directed the matches of the komusubi, sekiwake, ozeki, and yoko-zuna wrestlers to wear white *tabi*, or split-toed socks, and straw sandals.

Wrestlers of the New Era In 1959 Asashio Taro was promoted to yokozuna rank. At six feet two inches, he was a giant of a man, with chiseled features, thick eyebrows, and a chest full of hair. He was born in Kagoshima in 1929 and entered the Takasago stable at the age of eighteen. Unlike many tall wrestlers, he had a sound and steady technique, and he advanced steadily through the ranks until finally reaching the ozeki position in 1957 and that of yokozuna two years later. Persistent back trouble—Asashio was afflicted with separated vertebrae—kept him from becoming a record-breaking champion, for he was periodically forced to withdraw from tournaments. He retired in January 1962, four months before Wakanohana, and acted as a coach in the Takasago stable, under the elder name Furiwake, until assuming the position of master on the death of the former Takasago (Maedayama) in 1971.

The wrestlers most representative of the new era of phenomenal popularity that sumo was embarking on in the 1960s were Kashiwado Tsuyoshi and Taiho Koki. Both showed early promise, while fans and sumo association officials alike looked forward to their emergence in the makuuchi division from the time the two were apprentices. Kashiwado became a makuuchi wrestler in late 1958, and Taiho followed a year afterward. Similar in weight and stature, as well as in their weak point—pushing techniques—they soon dominated the sumo world.

Kashiwado was born in Yamagata Prefecture in 1938. He appeared in his first tournament at the age of fifteen under his real name, Togashi Tsuyoshi. Standing just over six feet one inch tall, but weighing a mere one hundred and seventy pounds, he worked steadily up the ranks until his advancement to the makuuchi division at the age of nineteen. The following spring he adopted the lineage name of the Isenoumi stable, Kashiwado, given only to potential champions and dating back to the mid-Edo period. He reached ozeki status following the Nagoya tournament of 1960. In September 1962 Kashiwado lost the title to Taiho in a play-off match for the championship, but following the tournament both ozeki were promoted to the yokozuna rank. Until 1963 the two wrestlers showed equal prowess, but a dislocated right shoulder early that year forced Kashiwado to withdraw from four tournaments. He won the fall tournament undefeated in an exciting comeback, but his record began to flag afterward. Kashiwado finally retired in July 1969 (by which time he weighed over three hundred and nine pounds) and began the Kagamiyama stable.

Taiho, born Naya Koki in 1940 in Karafuto (a northern island occupied by the Soviets now and known as Sakhalin), was the son of a White Russian refugee from the Bolshevik Revolution and a Japanese mother. In 1956, then living in Hokkaido with his mother, he was recruited by the Nishonoseki stable and appeared in his first professional tournament in the fall. Within three and a half years, when he was only twenty, he advanced to makuuchi status and won his first championship, at that time the youngest wrestler ever to be awarded the Emperor's Cup. In November 1960 he was promoted to ozeki rank, and in September 1961 he became the forty-eighth yokozuna, again the youngest wrestler yet to attain

49. *Taiho, who dominated the world of sumo in the 1960s, performs his ring-entering ceremony.*

that rank. Taiho's career at the top spanned the careers of seven other yokozuna: Wakanohana and Asashio, both of whom retired in 1962; Kashiwado, who became yokozuna with Taiho and retired in 1969; Tochinoumi Teruyoshi, who was promoted in 1964 and retired in 1966; Sadanoyama Shimmatsu, who was promoted in 1965 and retired in 1967; and Tamanoumi Masahiro and Kitanofuji Katsuaki, both of whom became yokozuna in 1970. Before himself retiring in 1971, Taiho won thirty-two championships—an all-time record—and came close to beating Futabayama's record of sixty-nine successive victories. A controversial ruling on the second day of the March tournament in Osaka in 1969 declared him the loser in a match with the maegashira wrestler Toda, stopping Taiho's winning streak at forty-five. The referee at first pointed his fan toward Taiho, but a discussion between the judges overruled that decision. Photographs published in the following day's paper proved the original decision to have been correct, for Toda's right foot had left the ring first. However, as tradition dictated, the judges' ruling held, although henceforth videotape machines were put into use for difficult cases. Taiho went on to twice win thirty-four successive matches, while two times he won six successive tournament championships, but he never again came near to breaking Futabayama's record. In the fall of 1969 the sumo association awarded him the honorary status of elder to commemorate his outstanding career, and in 1971 the champion retired to start a new stable.

The Naked Ambassadors By the mid-1960s Japan had not merely recovered from the devastation of World War II but was fast becoming a major economic power and beginning to be recognized by the rest of the world as such. In 1968 Japan's gross national product became the second largest among the non-Communist countries, and in 1973 Japan showed a favorable balance of trade that made it first in the world in terms of export production. In the political sphere, too, Japan reemerged as a power to be be reckoned with. Diplomatic relations were renewed with China in 1973, and the following year Gerald Ford became the first incumbent American president in history to visit Japan.

Sumo hit the international newsfront in the 1960s. In the summer of 1965—nearly sixty years after a group of Osaka wrestlers, inspired by Hitachiyama's highly touted tour of America and Europe in 1907–8, had first traveled to Russia—a number of wrestlers, led by Taiho, Sadanoyama, and Kashiwado, toured in the USSR at the invitation of the Soviet government. Praised on both fronts as the "naked ambassadors," the wrestlers were enthusiastically received during their goodwill performances at the National Circus Grounds in Moscow and in other regions of the country. Eight years later, in 1973, similar group of wrestlers traveled to Peking and Shanghai to commemorate the opening of Sino-Japanese relations.

The sumo world also began to become more accessible to foreigners during the 1960s. Probably the earliest attempt by a foreigner to gain entrance to the tight-knit society was in 1885, when the stablemaster Urakaze was reportedly approached by a huge American wrestler who pleaded to be taken on as a disciple. Urakaze, a bit astonished, submitted a letter to the government to inquire whether the man could be accepted as a trainee, but permission was denied on the grounds that there was no established system for allowing foreigners to reside permanently in the country. Sixty years later a foreign-born wrestler—Ozaki Kiichiro, an American Nisei from Colorado who managed to pass as a Japanese during the Second World War—successfully reached the top division of professional sumo, wrestling under the name Toyonishiki. And two years after that, Rikidozan, a Korean born in Nagasaki

50. *Takamiyama (Jesse Kuhaulua) takes on a group of children at a benefit performance.*

in 1924, advanced to makuuchi status as a member of the Nisho-noseki stable. He made it as far as the sekiwake rank before contracting lung trouble in late 1949. Monetary difficulties connected with his illness led to a fight with his stablemaster and his quitting sumo in September 1950. Rikidozan then turned to professional Western-style wrestling, where he became famous for his use of the karate chop. After touring the United States, he retired to promote wrestling in Tokyo and to manage a number of apartment buildings and nightclubs; in December 1963 he was stabbed to death in one of his bars by a gangster.

By the late 1970s over thirty non-Japanese wrestlers—most of them Japanese-born Koreans, but including a number of Hawaiians, mainland Americans, Brazilians, Chinese, and Tongans—had entered the ranks of professional sumo since the end of World War II. But few ever reached the top division, and only Takamiyama Daigoro, born Jesse Kuhaulua on the island of Maui, Hawaii, in June 1944, ever really became a star—and a superstar, at that. Sumo has been popular in Hawaii ever since Tachiyama and O-tori led a group of wrestlers to perform for the Japanese emigrants of Honolulu in 1914. A hiatus in professional tours to the islands was imposed by the Pacific War, but amateur Japanese groups began to travel to Hawaii to perform and to give instruction in the sport again in the early 1950s. In June 1962 a large group of professional wrestlers conducted their first major postwar tournament in Honolulu, which soon became a semiannual stop on the wrestlers' provincial tour circuit.

Jesse Kuhaulua joined the amateur Maui Sumo Club while in high school, primarily to strengthen his legs—which had been left weakened after he was hit by an automobile as a second grader—for football. In February 1964 the stablemaster Takasago (Maedayama), who was in charge of a group of makuuchi wrestlers stopping in Honolulu on their way to give exhibition matches in California, watched Jesse wrestle and was impressed enough to invite the Hawaiian to join his stable in Japan. Jesse, then not quite twenty years old, participated in his first professional sumo tournament in Osaka the following month under his real name but was afterward given the name Takamiyama, the original wrestling name of the stable's founder, Takasago Uragoro. Knowing no Japanese on his arrival in Japan but adapting with pertinacity to the harsh discipline of the sumo world, Takamiyama was put through a strict regimen of practice and advanced to juryo status following the January 1967 tournament. A year later he won the Fighting Spirit Award in his first tournament in the makuuchi division. In July 1972 Takamiyama became the first foreigner ever to win a tournament championship, and the then American ambassador to Japan, Robert Ingersoll, climbed up into the ring during the awards ceremony in Nagoya to read aloud a telegram of personal congratulations from Richard Nixon. Jesse, as he remained affectionately known to Japanese and foreigners alike, has at times reached over four hundred pounds on the scale. His height (almost six feet three inches) and weight often caused him to be caught off balance in the ring, for his legs never caught up with the rest of his body.

During the mid-1970s reactionary elements in the sumo association, startled by Takamiyama's unprecedented and unexpected success—he reached the sekiwake position many times—paved the way for an announcement by the association in September 1976 to the effect that, because sumo was the "national sport, recognized as such by the government," foreign-born sumo wrestlers would not be eligible to become elders after retirement. There was some public outcry, as two popular wrestlers were affected: Takamiyama and Kaneshiro, later called Tochihikari, a wrestler of Korean extraction. In 1980 Takamiyama acquired Japanese citizenship, taking his wife's surname to become Watanabe Daigoro. He appeared to be in fine condition as he neared his fortieth birthday, a remarkable age for an active sumo wrestler in the 1980s, but an injury to the left elbow in his fortieth year proved an insuperable handicap. Takamiyama dropped first from makuuchi to juryo, and then on down until he faced the unthinkable —demotion to the unsalaried makushita ranks. He retired as of the end of the May tournament in 1984, with his haircutting ceremony scheduled for February 3, 1985. He had spent twenty years in sumo, sixteen of them in the top division, and he holds a number of records, including those of 97 consecutive tournaments in makuuchi, and 1,399 bouts at that level. Also remarkable is his record number of twelve gold stars, *kimboshi*, awarded for beating a yokozuna. On retirement he assumed the elder name Azumazeki and became a trainer in the Takasago stable.

The Sumo World of the Seventies The program for the sumo tournament of 1967 permanently cut the number of wrestlers in the upper divisions by sixteen: six were eliminated from the makuuchi division to make a total of thirty-six, and ten from the juryo division to make twenty-eight. Sixteen sekitori, the cream of the sumo world, were suddenly lowered to the makushita division, a major drop in status that robbed these unfortunate men of the special privileges and salary that are allotted only to those of juryo and higher rank. The spring matches that year, taking place in full knowledge of the impending cuts, were desperately serious. Takamiyama, then in his first tournament as a juryo wrestler, won ten matches and remained in the juryo division, while his stablemate and senior, Maedayama, who went into the tournament three notches above him, was dropped to makushita status after winning only nine.

In December 1968, almost immediately after taking part in the award ceremonies of the Kyushu tournament, Tokitsukaze (the former Futabayama), then director-in-chief of the sumo association, died in a Tokyo hospital of hepatitis complications at the age of fifty-six. The master of the Dewanoumi stable (the former maegashira Dewanohana Yoshihide) was elected director-in-chief. As such, he resumed the name he had used earlier as a coach, and his son-in-law, the yokozuna Sadanoyama, immediately retired and took over the position of stablemaster in his place. A year later Kashiwado retired. Taiho, on the other hand, began his famous winning streak in the fall of 1968, only to be stopped by the notorious false decision in favor of Toda in March 1969. Kitanofuji and Tamanoumi were promoted to yokozuna status the following January, and during the May tournament of 1971 Taiho retired.

Tamanoumi Masahiro, born in 1944 in Aichi Prefecture, entered the Nishonoseki stable at the age of fifteen, but in the summer of 1962 he left with the Nishonoseki coach Kataonami (the former Tamanoumi) when the latter began his own stable. Less than a year after becoming a makuuchi wrestler, he downed Taiho and went on to rack up a steady record of successes that led to his promotion to ozeki in 1966 and yokozuna in 1970. He had won six championships when he died unexpectedly of an embolism after apparently successful surgery for neglected appendicitis in October 1971. Until Tamanoumi's death a wrestler unable to appear in a match because of sickness or injury was judged as losing, and many wrestlers, including Tamanoumi, customarily attended tournaments even when seriously ill in an attempt to stave off the run of defaults that would bring about a demotion in rank. It transpired that Tamanoumi had been suffering from other serious ailments for years—ailments that he could not afford to take time off to have treated. The shock of this revelation was a major factor in the eventual establishment of an accident system that allowed a man who was injured during a tournament to stay out of the following matches without having any losses counted against him.

Kitanofuji Katsuaki, born in 1942 in Hokkaido, became a member of the Dewanoumi stable in 1957. In 1964 he reached the makuuchi division and was promoted to ozeki status two and a half years later. In early 1967 he left the Dewanoumi stable to join the newly formed Kokonoe stable, and he won his first championship two months later. With Tamanoumi, he was promoted to yokozuna rank in January 1970. As Taiho began to show the strain of his long years in the ring, the rivalry between "Kita" and "Tama" dominated the sumo world until Tamanoumi's death, following which Kitanofuji went into a slump. Reportedly suffering from insomnia, he withdrew halfway through the May tournament the following year. After his recovery he faced the yokozuna Kotozakura and Wajima until his retirement in 1974. He opened his own Izutsu stable, but on the death of his mentor, the former Chiyonoyama, he took over his name, Kokonoe, and his wrestlers, adding them to his own. The Izutsu name was taken over by the elder Kimigahama, who had wrestled under the name Tsurugamine. His Kimigahama stable thereupon changed, in name only, to Izutsu.

Kotozakura Masakatsu was promoted to yokozuna rank after the January tournament in 1973. Born in 1940 in Tottori Prefecture, he made his first tournament appearance in early 1959 as a member of the Sadogatake stable. He advanced to the maku-

51.　*Wajima throwing salt into the ring.*

uchi division in 1963, and reached komusubi rank, when an injury to his right ankle caused him to drop to juryo status before he could recover. He was promoted to ozeki rank in 1967 and remained in that position for over five years. Just when everyone thought that his career as a wrestler was finished, Kotozakura suddenly won two successive tournaments and was promoted to yokozuna rank in late January 1973. He weighed well over three hundred pounds, had a tremendous belly, and was possessed of a charging power so great that other wrestlers said that it was like having a mountain crag dropped on them. He was already thirty-two years old when advanced to the yokozuna position, and in 1974, after only eight tournaments as grand champion, he retired. His stablemaster died only ten days after the announcement, and Kotozakura immediately became the new master of the Sadogatake stable.

With Kotozakura's retirement, the attention of the sumo world turned to Wajima Hiroshi and Kitanoumi Toshimitsu. Wajima, the first college graduate ever to become yokozuna, was born in 1948 in Ishikawa Prefecture. He was a star member of his high school wrestling team and, as a student at Nihon Daigaku (Japan University) in Tokyo, he won the national collegiate sumo championship two years in a row. He was recruited by the Hanakago

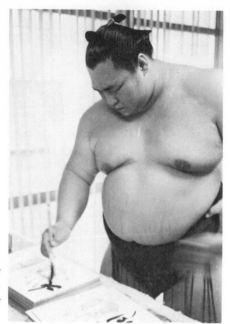

52. *Kitanoumi signing his name on cards that bear his handprint. A typical memento, these are sold to a wrestler's fans.*

stable before his graduation from the university and performed in his first professional tournament as a makushita wrestler in January 1970. A year later Wajima—his real name—advanced to the makuuchi division. His promotion to ozeki status in November 1972 and to yokozuna in May 1973 surprised no one. An injury in March 1975 forced him to quit halfway through the tournament and to miss most of the May and all of the July matches that year, but it was not too long before he was able to make a comeback. He won his thirteenth championship in July 1979—his first since November 1977—and it proved that at thirty-one he could still successfully challenge the seemingly total domination of the ring by Kitanoumi. He retired in March 1981 and succeeded his father-in-law as master of the Hanakago stable.

Born in Hokkaido in 1953, Kitanoumi was only thirteen when he joined the Mihogaseki stable in 1967, and at first combined training with attending the local junior high school. He left school without graduating, and in March 1969 he advanced to makushita status, still at the age of only fifteen. He reached juryo rank just before his eighteenth birthday, and seven months later advanced to the makuuchi—breaking Taiho's record as the youngest man to be promoted to makuuchi status. He broke another record of

Taiho's by being promoted to yokozuna at the age of twenty-one years and two months in July 1974 (Taiho had been about one month older). In the summer of 1972, five years after Kitanoumi began his career, a ruling was introduced prohibiting boys from participating in professional sumo tournaments until they had graduated from junior high school, thus making it almost impossible for any wrestler ever to beat these records. As yokozuna, Kitanoumi was not only one of the largest wrestlers in the ring, weighing well over three hundred sixty pounds, but in his prime was unquestionably the strongest. He was a true celebrity, whose marriage to the daughter of a restaurateur following the September 1978 tournament was widely publicized. In all, he won twenty-four championships, seven of them without a loss. The later years of his career, however, were marred by injury, poor performances, and withdrawals—except for one final no-loss championship in May 1984. His retirement was announced in January 1985.

In 1977 Wakamisugi Toshihito emerged as a challenger to Kitanoumi's reign. Born in 1953 in Aomori Prefecture, he began wrestling in 1968 as a member of the Futagoyama stable. He was still a makushita wrestler in 1972 when his stablemate Takanohana rose to the rank of ozeki. The next year, however, he entered the makuuchi division himself, and in 1975 he was promoted to komusubi rank. He became an ozeki after the January 1977 tournament, and although he won only one championship, in the summer of that year, he was promoted to yokozuna in May 1978 after amassing a total of forty wins during three tournaments, a record superior to those of the previous thirteen yokozuna at the time of their promotions. A week after the announcement of his promotion, Wakamisugi changed his name to Wakanohana Kanji, the wrestling name of his master, Futagoyama. With sweet, almost feminine features and a well-proportioned frame, he was extremely popular, and numbered many women among his fans. In his health, however, and in his private life—his marriage to his stablemaster's daughter ended before long in divorce—he was unlucky, and 1983 saw his retirement at the early age of twenty-nine after a disappointing yokozuna career.

Mienoumi Tsuyoshi had just completed his ninety-seventh tournament as a professional wrestler when, at the age of thirty-one, he joined Wajima, Kitanoumi, and Wakanohana as yokozuna in the summer of 1979. Born in 1948, he entered the Dewanoumi stable in 1963 under his own name, Ishiyama, but three years later adopted a professional name derived from his home prefecture, Mie. He advanced to the makuuchi division in 1969, and a year later, as komusubi, he downed two yokozuna, Taiho and Tamano-umi. In July 1972, as a sekiwake, he was forced to drop out of the tournament with an attack of hepatitis, and four years later, just six months after becoming an ozeki, injury caused him to quit midway through both the March and May tournaments and he fell back to sekiwake status. Although he regained the ozeki rank that July, it took three more years before his record was good enough for promotion to the yokozuna rank. At last, in spite of his advancing age, he achieved his promotion following the Nagoya tournament of 1979. He retired after only seven tournaments as yokozuna, however, and shortly after opened his own Musashigawa stable, having bought the name from the retiring Musashigawa.

The yokozuna were not the only stars of the ring in the 1970s. Takamiyama, the Hawaiian wrestler mentioned earlier, rose as high as sekiwake and was also much in demand for television commercials and advertising posters. The ozeki Asahikuni Masuo, in spite of his diminutive size, put in a solid performance for years on end, eventually retiring in 1979, whereupon he founded his own Oshima stable. By 1984 he had gathered so many young wrestlers that a larger stable had to be built. Kaiketsu Masateru (Hanakago stable), twice promoted to ozeki and twice demoted to the lower sanyaku ranks, won the championship as a komusubi in November 1974 by beating Kitanoumi in a play-off, and won a championship in September 1976 after being demoted to maegashira. The ozeki Takanohana Toshiaki (Futagoyama stable), handsome and trim at two hundred and thirty pounds, in the same mold as his older brother and stablemaster, the former yokozuna Wakanohana I, beat Kitanofuji twice during the early 1970s and won two championships as ozeki in 1975. Early in the decade he was called the "Prince of the Sumo World," but by late 1978, overtaken in his bid for yokozuna promotion by his junior, Wakamisugi, he became known as the "Eternal Ozeki," as his dreams of succeeding his brother faded rapidly. His retirement came in January 1981, still at the ozeki rank, but without doubt Takanohana will go down in sumo history as one of the most popular and appealing wrestlers of all time. He has now opened a new stable, Fujishima.

In the Mid-Eighties The world of sumo is in constant flux. While some things change hardly at all, and some "innovations"—such as the rule that both wrestlers must touch the ground with both hands before the initial charge—are really reintroductions of customs which had been allowed to lapse, the wrestlers themselves, and the performances of individuals, show such variation that the task of the sumo writer is Sisyphean. A twenty-year-old hailed as a future Taiho sinks without trace or flounders in juryo for ten years. A plodder suddenly catches fire at the age of thirty. A fracture or a bad sprain hampers or even wrecks a promising career. And always at the bottom of the heap there are the teenage boys who join a stable in high hope and who—mostly—drop out within a year or two. The only certain things are the records and the retirements, especially the latter, for when once a man retires, he is credited forever with the highest rank he has ever possessed. Let us finish this chapter, then, with a glance at some important retirements of the 1980s. Dates given will be those of the haircutting ceremony, which takes place some months after the man actually retires from competition.

May 1981 saw the retirement ceremony (*intai-zumo*) of Takanohana, mentioned just above, and also of the late-blooming yokozuna Mienoumi. In early October, following the autumn tournament, ozeki Masuiyama, son of a former ozeki Masuiyama, formally retired. (In 1984, his father reached the retirement age set for sumo elders, and so he took over as the master of the Mihogaseki stable.) The day after Masuiyama's intai-zumo saw that of one of the all-time greats: Wajima. For several months, Wajima, who had retained his real name throughout his wrestling career, had been Hanakago stablemaster. His topknot received the final cut, not from his predecessor, who had died shortly before the ceremony, but from the elder Futagoyama, who himself had belonged to the Hanakago stable before founding his own. The year 1981 saw, besides these retirements, Chiyonofuji become yokozuna and Takanosato making a strong bid for ozeki status, which in fact came to him after the January tournament in 1982.

At the same time that Takanosato was becoming an ozeki, the veterans Arase and Yutakayama were going through their haircutting ceremonies. Indeed, 1982 was veterans' year; Kurohimeyama, Tamanofuji, and Yoshinotani held retirement ceremonies in May, the first two in the Kokugikan, the last, privately. In the January tournament, which was his last, Kurohimeyama had been the last active wrestler who had beaten Taiho; and when college champion Nagaoka, later to become ozeki Asashio, was roaring up through the makushita and juryo ranks in a seemingly unstoppable progress, Yoshinotani was the first man to beat him in professional sumo. Daigo, a former bow-twirling specialist, retired in September. Earlier in the same month, a promising young Hawaiian of Samoan ancestry, Salevaa Atisanoe, made his first appearance on the ranking list. His sumo name was Konishiki, and in

53. The young Hawaiian-Samoan wrestler Konishiki receives careful instructions from Takasago oyakata, the former Asashio Taro, in the Takasago stable keikoba.

May 1984 he astonished the sumo world by a strong runner-up performance.

Asashio, Wakashimazu, and Hokutenyu all attained ozeki status in 1983, and Takanosato was elevated to yokozuna in July. The most important intai-zumo was that of the hapless Wakanohana II in May. With a new wife and baby daughter, he made a fresh start as Magaki oyakata, and eventually founded a stable of his own in early 1984. In May 1983 there was also an unusual triple ceremony to celebrate the retirements of three men of the Tokitsukaze stable. The most successful of them was Futatsuryu, who would have rated a ceremony of his own, but his stablemate Yamaguchi, who had had some success as Taniarashi but had reverted to his real name as he slipped down the ranking list, joined him. The third man, Makimoto, did not technically rate a Kokugikan ceremony, as most of his career had been spent at the makushita level; but his age at retirement was forty-one, giving him a longer active career than any other wrestler in modern times.

From the vantage point of 1985, one phenomenon that could hardly have been expected a few years ago was the emergence of Chiyonofuji, a native of Hokkaido and a member of the Kokonoe stable, as a great yokozuna. Although from the beginning he

54. A triumphant Chiyonofuji holds aloft the championship trophy that he won in the January 1985 tournament, the first in the new Ryogoku Kokugikan.

showed the fighting spirit that won him the nickname "the Wolf," his slight build combined with a frequently dislocated shoulder gave him an uneven record for some years. But he added ten kilograms and with a weight-training program developed great physical strength. He was the first wrestler to win' the Emperor's Cup in the new Ryogoku Kokugikan, with a fifteen to zero record that gave him his eleventh tournament.

In the 1980s, the phenomenal popularity sumo witnessed during the latter half of the 1970s shows no indication of abating. Instead, interest in this ancient sport continues to increase. The world of sumo, along with the other traditional entertainments of Kabuki, Bunraku and Noh, is acknowledged to be one of the last bastions of the feudalistic mores and rituals of the Edo period. A century ago it was considered too vulgar for the pro-Western tastes of the Meiji-era elite, but widespread nostalgia and a revived respect for Japan's past, both nationally and internationally, have resulted today in unprecedented enthusiasm for sumo. Although pessimistic critics in the late 1960s foretold a steady decline in support for sumo as baseball usurped the traditional foundations of its popularity and fewer boys risked the economic uncertainties and rigorous training of professional sumo, fulfillment of this gloomy prediction has not come true. The opening of the new Kokugikan in January 1985 drew capacity crowds, and many who wanted to go were obliged to watch on television instead. The financial insecurity and physical hardships of the life of a wrestler, which ought to hold few attractions for the youth of a prospering Japan, seem to be counterbalanced by the fortune and fame that accompany success in the ring and continue to encourage a steady flow of aspiring youths to the Tokyo stables.

Sumo Today

5. Wrestlers and Stables

Ranking of Wrestlers The half square mile situated to the south of Ryogoku Station in Tokyo has been known as the sumo district since the middle of the Edo period. Next to the trim modern buildings of the still-famous Eko-in temple, venue of tournaments from the mid-eighteenth to the early twentieth century, there is a flat piece of ground that is the site of the old Kokugikan. Rebuilt after World War II, and having served as an auditorium for Nihon University, it was finally razed in April 1983. As of 1984 the site was being used as a parking lot, pending the erection of a museum of the Edo period.

Over half of the thirty-odd sumo training stables, or heya, some of which were founded over two hundred years ago, lie scattered through the district: the Dewanoumi, Izutsu, Kasugano, Mihogaseki, Nishonoseki, Oshima, Tatsutagawa, Tatsunami, Tokitsukaze, and Wakamatsu stables are all located within blocks of each other. Most of the stables founded in the last few decades were able to find land only some distance away from the sumo district. Hanakago stable was founded out to the west at Asagaya, and its success encouraged other would-be stablemasters to look farther afield. Nevertheless, Ryogoku continues to exert its old attraction, and the Kokonoe stable managed to move back into the area from Edogawa ward. The practice of *de-geiko,* of wrestlers visiting neighboring stables to train together, is a valuable means of honing skills, and an isolated stable is at a disadvantage. There is constant change. Not so long ago one of the most respected old stables, the Takasago, was forced by problems with its land deeds to relocate near Asakusabashi Station, though this is only just across the Sumida River from Ryogoku.

Life in the stables revolves on traditions, developed and nurtured over the centuries, of absolute obedience to and respect for superiors. Each wrestler must acknowledge the prerogatives of higher rank and act accordingly. The strict hierarchy of the sumo world, although seemingly outdated and feudalistic, is actually a fundamentally meritocratic one, for it is founded solely on individual ability. Rank is a reflection of a wrestler's success and nothing else, and rank is the only important consideration. It dictates how a wrestler will dress, what his wages will be, and how he will be treated by other members of the sumo world.

The system employed to rank the over seven hundred professional wrestlers who take part in the national tournaments can be visualized as a pyramid-shaped hierarchy:

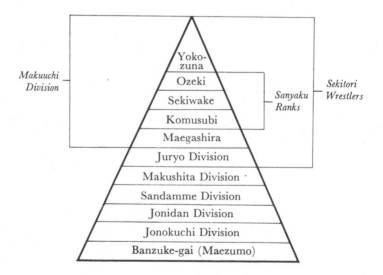

By far the greater number of wrestlers can be found in the lower ranks.

At the top is the makunouchi, or makuuchi, division, comprising five ranks: yokozuna, ozeki, sekiwake, komusubi, and maegashira. The number of yokozuna and ozeki is determined by the number of wrestlers qualified to hold the rank, and usually varies from one to four; exceptionally, there have been five yokozuna for a very short period. It has happened that a man with a good record has been passed over because there were already enough yokozuna, however, while when they were in short supply, a man with a less distinguished record has been promoted. There are normally two sekiwake and two komusubi. The number of margashira fluctuates between twenty-four and twenty-eight to keep the number of makuuchi wrestlers nearly constant at thirty-six. There have, however, been many changes in the numbers, and doubtless there will continue to be experimentation. The figures given below are according to the program for the January 1985 tournament. The titleholders, that is, the ranks of komusubi upwards, are collectively referred to as sanyaku, or three ranks. The yokozuna title, created in the late eighteenth century, was not officially considered a ranking until the early twentieth century. The term sekitori is used to refer to a wrestler of either the makuuchi or the next lower division, the juryo. There are twenty-six wrestlers in the juryo division. The name derives from the amount formerly paid to the *jumaime*, the first ten wrestlers listed in the second row of the program; *ju* means ten and *ryo* was an old unit of currency.

In descending order of rank below the juryo are the makushita, with 120 wrestlers; the sandamme, with 200; the jonidan, with 278 and finally, the jonokuchi, with 78. Novice wrestlers, who are not listed on the ranking list but who also appear in the tournaments, are known as *banzuki gai*, outside the list, and their bouts, because they are not yet professionals, are called *maezumo*, preliminary sumo. Wrestlers of makushita rank and below (apart from the unlisted boys, who are a special case) appear on only seven days of each fifteen-day tournament. Sekitori wrestlers have a bout on every day of the tournament.

Wrestlers of the lower ranks, that is, makushita and below, wear in the ring the same plain dark cotton belts they wear for training. Those of juryo and makuuchi ranks, however, wear white cotton belts for training and have costly belts of satin for tournament appearances. These were formerly dark-colored, but since the advent of color television many wrestlers have favored bright colors. Whatever the material, the *sagari*, a decorative fringe, is tucked into the front of the belt and worn by all during a tournament, though not for training. Outside the sumo hall, the dress code varies from stable to stable, but in winter a sandamme youth is commonly allowed to wear for the first time the *haori*, a knee-length overcoat, over his kimono. Those below that rank must do without a coat whatever the weather.

For formal occasions, which include tournament appearances, the makuuchi and juryo wrestlers wear their long, oiled hair in a style known as *oicho*, or gingko leaf; a small circle is shaved on the crown of the head, and the hair is pulled back, tied with a paper string called a *motoi*, and doubled forward in a neat queue, fanning slightly at the very front. With an instrument resembling an old-fashioned steel knitting needle, the hairdresser, called *tokoyama*, gently draws out the hair from the scalp into a bag shape, and finally shapes it into a sharp edge that stands out from the side of the face and the back of the neck. All lower-ranking wrestlers— and sekitori too, on an ordinary, day-to-day basis—have their hair fashioned in a *chommage*, a simpler style drawn tight against the head and with no fanning of the queue. Both these styles were adopted from fashions popular in the middle of the Edo period. In the early 1870s, short Western-style haircuts became the vogue. One of the popular phrases of the day was, "If you knock on a close-clipped head you hear the sound of civilization." Barbers catering to the old Edo topknots disappeared, and as sumo wrestlers alone were permitted to keep their crowning glory, they had to borrow hairdressers from the Kabuki theater. Eventually the professional sumo hairdresser, the tokoyama, evolved. Not all stables have their own tokoyama, but most have at least one, and some of the large stables have three or even four. During tournament time these will attend to men of other stables, while for the easy-to-dress chommage, the wrestlers themselves can do one another's hair in a pinch.

A wrestler's treatment in his stable also depends largely on his rank, although the question of seniority by age and experience— the principle by which the rest of Japanese society is guided—can be a touchy problem when a younger wrestler advances to a division that is higher than that of a man who has been in the stable longer.

Apprentices rise at dawn to begin chores around the building and do their warm-up exercises in the practice ring. The hardest and dirtiest jobs naturally go to the most junior of them, a strong incentive to strive for promotion. The stablemaster assigns individuals as *tsukebito*, (literally, attendants, but in effect personal servants) to himself, the coaches, and the sekitori; they are also the cleaners and the cooks; they put out the garbage and walk the dog. A derogatory name for them used to be *fundoshi katsugi*, or loincloth carriers, for one of their tasks is to carry on their shoulders the boxes containing their seniors' tournament clothes. In the larger stables, the pyramidal structure is more noticeable, but anywhere, the small privileges of seniority are jealously guarded. In general, wrestlers will advise and teach those two ranks below themselves, so in this way the sandamme, though still low compared with the sekitori, will enjoy displaying their seniority to the jonokuchi apprentices.

Once a wrestler makes the juryo rank, thereby becoming a sekitori, all of his daily needs are provided for: he is assigned at least one junior to act as his personal servant; he is assisted in dressing; his back is scrubbed for him in the bath; he can have his telephone calls answered and errands run for him; in rainy weather, he even has a paper umbrella held over his head. The higher his sekitori rank, the more assistants a wrestler will have. Meals, too, are taken by order of rank, beginning with the highest-ranked men in the stable, who are served by those of the lowest ranks.

Stable Regimen When a wrestler is not on tour or participating in a tournament, his daily stable regimen seldom varies. Apprentices in their first six months go off to the sumo school at the Kokugikan, where they spend a grueling morning in physical exercise under the direction of two elders assisted by experienced makushita men who are assigned to do a stint of this work. After basic training in such things as learning how to fall, the boys clean up and then attend some academic lessons: history of sumo, traditional singing, and calligraphy—at least enough to enable them to write a stylish autograph. The boys who have passed through this basic training will join the regular sessions in their own stables. Like everything else, these go according to rank.

Wrestlers of the lowest division enter the ring first, under the eyes of the sandamme and perhaps one or two makushita wrestlers. Two youths fight; the loser leaves the ring; the winner is besieged by the rest; he chooses his next opponent, and the bout begins immediately. Training in general is called *keiko,* or *-geiko* in compound words. The form of training just described is called *moshiai-geiko,* and it will be seen that boys who win get much more practice than those who lose, thus becoming more proficient, so that they win even more often. When the time for that division's training is nearly over, another kind of bout, called *butsukari-geiko,* gets under way. A senior, preferably bigger and heavier, stands in the ring and the junior charges at him from outside, trying desperately to push him across the ring and out the other side. At the end of this exercise, the youngsters move to one side or, on nice days, out into the

55. *Fujizakura, in white, gives butsukari-geiko practice to a junior in the Takasago stable.*

street, to do their winding-down exercises, after which they start cleaning, go shopping, or begin work in the kitchen. Two apprentices sweep the ring to freshen the surface, and then the whole process begins again with the next division.

Wrestlers present themselves in the *keikoba*, or training area, when those two divisions their junior are training. They may begin their own private exercises immediately, or they may stand at the side of the ring and shout advice. Meanwhile, the stablemaster and the coaches arrive. In a small or new stable, the master may well have been there from the very beginning. The master or coach may don the white cotton practice belt he used when he was an active wrestler; then he can be distinguished from the sekitori only by his modern hairstyle. Upstairs in their private rooms (sekitori wrestlers usually have rooms to themselves, while juniors share communal rooms) the juryo and makuuchi men begin to stir beneath their bedclothes, and their tsukebito bring up their white practice belts and help them dress. Married sekitori, who are required to live nearby, arrive at the same time by car or bicycle. By eight o'clock the sekitori descend to the training area, where they bow at the door to the stablemaster and move to the ringside amid a murmur of respectful greetings from their juniors. Although the sekitori will probably not enter the ring for another hour, this is the time for visitors to come in and take their seats in the observation area raised above the training space.

The exercises done by the wrestlers during the daily practice session are designed, as it is often said, to exceed the limits of the flesh and strengthen the wrestler's spirit. The intensity with which the exercises are practiced depends on the individual, but every day most wrestlers are expected to do at least one hundred shiko, lifting their legs alternately as high and as straight in the air to the side as possible, then slamming the foot down on the earth of the practice area, palms pressed hard on the knees. The shiko strengthens and makes pliable the muscles and joints of the knees and hips. To stretch those same muscles, wrestlers squat with their hands on their knees and extend one leg at a time straight out to the side. They may also do frog-hops from the same squatting position. Another stretching exercise, known as *matawari*, or thigh split, is considered the most painful of all exercises. To do this, the wrestler must sit on the ground and spread his legs wide, preferably straight out to the sides, and then bend forward until his chest touches the ground. Apprentices must usually be helped in this by older wrestlers or coaches, who push down on their backs and hold their legs down until they succeed in reaching the earth. *Teppo* is an exercise designed to strengthen the arms and shoulders and help coordinate footwork: the wrestler faces an upright wooden pillar and with a slow rhythmic movement slams each hand in turn against the pillar at chest level, exhaling on each stroke and gently swishing the foot on the same side across in front of the other foot.

When the turn of the sekitori finally comes, another form of practice, called *samban-geiko*, is more common. In this, the same two men face each other in a long series of bouts. Samban-geiko is also common between two wrestlers of about one rank apart—a valuable opportunity for the junior to improve his skill, and a useful warm-up for the senior. The sekitori bouts are watched closely by the very young apprentices, who have returned by now from their chores. They stand outside the ring holding towels, ready to brush off their assigned seniors, and equally ready to learn the finer points by watching the experts. The whole session ends at ten or eleven o'clock, when all the juniors get back into the ring for another short stint of vigorous muscle-stretching exercises, after which everybody heads for the bath and the hairdresser—in descending order of rank.

When the sekitori practice is at its height, the stable cooks—alternating groups of lower-ranking wrestlers—begin to prepare the first and main meal of the day. Wrestlers eat only two meals a day and spend at least one of these sitting around a bubbling pot of *chanko nabe*. In the world of sumo, any dish cooked in the *nabe* style—stewed in and eaten directly from the nabe, a deep, covered cooking pot heated on a gas ring—is referred to as *chanko*. The word is thought to come from the Nagasaki dialect, with *chan* meaning Chinese and *ko* being a Chinese word for the cooking pot. There are other, considerably less likely, theories.

Meals in a stable are always taken after training, never before. Wrestling with a full stomach dulls a wrestler's sensitivity, and besides, in a violent practice bout many find themselves flung bodily to the ground. An unfortunately placed sharp blow to the mid-section after a meal could be dangerous. Stable tradition from ages past has dictated, therefore, that wrestlers eat no breakfast. After a heavy workout on an empty stomach, most of the stable occupants have worked up a hearty appetite. The youngsters trying to gain weight force themselves to eat four or five bowls of rice, and some of their seniors have gargantuan appetites, even though it is in their interest to eat moderately when once they have reached their optimum weight. Some are, indeed, careful eaters; but there are too many well-attested stories of prodigious consumption for this aspect of sumo life to be dismissed as mere myth. The chanko-nabe itself is a hearty stew of meat or fish, tofu, and vegetables, and is accompanied by an attractive assortment of dips for each mouthful.

Wrestlers eat by turns according, of course, to rank. The lowest ranks, who were up and working before anyone else, must patiently and hungrily wait until all of the others have finished and gone upstairs to rest. Afternoon naps often last for several hours, and it is this inactivity following the heavy meal that is the true shaper of the wrestler's bulging stomach. The stable is generally quiet during the rest of the day. Some of the wrestlers go out to play golf or seek other entertainment; popular ones are called on by admirers, who take them out for their evening meal. The married sekitori are free to go home after the noon meal. The evening meal in the stable is therefore a quiet affair of unspectacular food provided for those who are left with nothing better to do. Even for those out on the town, however, the next morning's practice session looms, and they usually return quite early, in time to get a good night's sleep.

Elders and Stable Management All professional wrestlers must be members of one of the stables, which are run and managed by retired wrestlers known as *shisho*, or masters. The stablemasters are part of the 105 elders, who, together with the active wrestlers, the referees, the announcers, and the coaches, form the Japan Sumo Association. This organization—the official name is Zaidan Hojin Nihon Sumo Kyokai—is divided into a number of committees, each staffed by elders elected to the positions, which supervise virtually every aspect of professional sumo. At the very top is a ten-member board of directors made up mostly of influential stablemasters and headed by a director-in-chief, or president. The board itself is subject to the review of a council of trustees, which consists of all the elders, four representatives chosen from the wrestlers, and two referees.

Elder names (*toshiyori mei*), which have always been hereditary and have been limited to their present number since the consolidation of the Tokyo and Osaka sumo associations in 1926—at that time seventeen elder names from Osaka were added to the eighty-eight of Tokyo—can be assumed only when a wrestler retires from the ring. During the Edo period, a wrestler or referee of any rank could continue the elder line of his master, but in the twentieth century, requirements became increasingly stringent. In the early 1920s it was announced that only wrestlers of juryo rank or higher and referees from these same divisions were eligible for elder status. In 1951 the hereditary line of Negishi, which had been in charge of lettering the ranking list from the mid-eighteenth century, was dissolved, and seven years later referees were prohibited from becoming elders.

In order to succeed to an elder position today, a wrestler must have participated in at least one tournament in the makuuchi rank or have wrestled twenty consecutive tournaments or a total of twenty-five as a juryo wrestler. In addition, he must obtain a transfer of the stock held by an elder (*toshiyori kabu*) from someone who is approaching the association's mandatory retirement age of sixty-five, or from the family of a deceased elder. In theory, a man assuming the position is obliged to support the family of the man he succeeds, but in practice a one-time cash settlement is made for the stock. Since substantial salaries and other benefits are guaranteed an elder for life by the association, the stock is both difficult and expensive to obtain. When sumo's popularity and profits grew in the late 1950s, so did the status and financial benefits of being an elder of the sumo association. Hoarding of the elder stocks increased sharply, and by the early 1960s a position cost around ten million yen; today it may be seven or eight times that. With the enforcement of a mandatory retirement age in 1961, the purchase of stock became a bit easier, but even so there are always many more wrestlers willing to buy than there are positions available. Waiting for an elder's stock to come on the market has even caused a man to suffer the disgrace of repeated demotions, as happened in the case of ex-ozeki Daiju, who fought—and lost—in the juryo division in May 1977.

Men who wish to become elders try to make arrangements for transfer of stock long before they expect to retire from the ring. It is not uncommon for a man with no stock of his own to borrow it from a still-active wrestler who already has it, paying a rental fee for the privilege until he is able to acquire his own, or until the real owner retires from the ring and needs the position himself. Those wrestlers who fail to buy stock must ultimately leave the sumo world and rejoin the general public—unless, of course, they are employed by a stablemaster in some capacity.

Any wrestler who becomes an elder is eligible in theory to become the owner of a training stable. There are thus a potential 105 stables, although the actual number in September 1984 was only 37. Elders who are not stablemasters are affiliated with one of the stables as advisers or coaches. All elders, including stablemasters, have the title *oyakata* attached to their name, and are regularly addressed as "Oyakata." Normally, when a master dies or retires, a former or current member of his stable will inherit the elder name and position of the master, and there is often a good chance for a coach to succeed as stablemaster. On occasion a coach who finds such prospects thwarted will gain permission from the master to take a number of the stable's wrestlers, those who joined that particular stable on his account, and begin his own new stable. In 1960 there was temporary confusion as to who would succeed to the mastership of the Dewanoumi stable following the death of the seventh-generation Dewanoumi (the former yokozuna Tsunenohana), but at length the coach Musashigawa (the former Dewanohana, maegashira wrestler of the late 1950s) took over. The wrestler Sadanoyama later married Musashigawa's daughter and then sealed his future as the next Dewanoumi when he was promoted to yokozuna status in 1965. In spite of a longstanding Dewanoumi tradition of discouraging its wrestlers from going to other stables after retirement, the coach Kokonoe (the former yokozuna Chiyonoyama), seeing his last hopes of becoming master himself dashed, broke away in early 1967 to begin the Kokonoe stable, taking with him Kitanofuji (an ozeki at that time) and nine other Dewanoumi wrestlers.

A retired wrestler beginning a new stable normally maintains close ties with one that is larger and more firmly established. These familial groups are called *ichimon*, literally, "one gate," and until 1965 wrestlers from the same ichimon were not matched together in tournaments. Now, however, only wrestlers from the same stable are not matched except in the very rare instance of a play-off between stablemates. The Dewanoumi ichimon at present consists of the Dewanoumi, Kasugano, Mihogaseki, and Musashigawa stables. The Nishonoseki-Hanakago ichimon comprises, besides those two, Futagoyama, Taiho, Kataonami, Sadogatake, Hanaregoma, Fujishima, and Oshiogawa stables, as well as the newest stable, Magaki. The Tatsunami-Isegahama ichimon contains also the Kasugayama, Miyagino, Tomozuna, Asahiyama, Ajikawa, Kumagatani, Kise, Onaruto, and Oshima stables. Not all new stables spring directly from the head of the ichimon; the Onaruto stable is an offshoot of the Asahiyama, for instance. Moreover, a new stablemaster may be welcomed into another ichimon if he has left his former stable on bad terms with the master. Thus Kokonoe, although founded by a wrestler from the Dewanoumi stable, went into the Takasago group, which also includes Takadagawa, Wakamatsu, and Oyama. The remaining stable family, the Tokitsukaze ichimon, contains Kagamiyama, Tatsutagawa, Isenoumi, Michinoku, and Izutsu stables and the new Minato stable.

In the case of a new stablemaster, substantial fees are paid not only for the elder stock but for the land and buildings as well. If he cannot afford to buy up all of the property of his predecessor, he may make up a contract with the relatives of the former master to pay monthly rental fees for the stable facilities. Such agreements have led to disastrous complications in the past. In late 1975 the Asahiyama stablemaster died suddenly, leaving the succession unclear. Of the two most suitable candidates, Kotetsuyama left and set up his own Onaruto stable, and the widow tentatively designated the other, Wakafutase, as her husband's successor to the stable. As he could not afford to purchase the name or the property outright, Wakafutase arranged to pay a sizable monthly fee to rent the stable and borrow the name for five years. When Wakafutase had already been recognized as stablemaster by the sumo association, however, another wrestler, still active, made an offer as a result of which the widow tried to retract her contract and set up a new master. In the eyes of the association Wakafutase was still the master, but was obliged to vacate the stable premises and move out with his wrestlers. Six of them, however, all foreigners from Tonga in Micronesia, refused. In this case the sumo association was obliged to accept their resignation, as they had by their own action become unattached. This cut short a promising new chapter of sumo history.

In May 1941 a system was established whereby a retiring yokozuna could become an honorary one-generation elder under his own wrestling name. When he died or retired from the world of sumo, his elder position was to be dissolved, and thus it could not be passed on to a successor. This system was abolished in 1958, being replaced by one in which a yokozuna who found it impossible to obtain stock could become an honorary elder for five years, receiving a salary as an officer of the association. If after those five years, however, the former champion had failed to acquire permanent elder stock, he would be forced to retire. In recent years the sole exception to this rule was the great Taiho. He retired from the ring in 1971 and was permitted by the association to become a one-generation elder. On his retirement in 1985, Kitanoumi was granted the same privilege, so that at present there are actually 107 elder positions; elsewhere in this book, however, the regular number of 105 has been adhered to.

In addition to the elders, there are a limited number of associate-elder positions open to retired wrestlers of makushita rank. Eight *wakaimono-gashira* (youth leaders) assist during the tournaments by marshaling the beginners, keeping a record of their scores, and generally seeing that they know what to do. They are usually given permanent assignments as coaches to the larger stables. There are also eight *sewanin* (assistants) who take charge of equipment and help collect tickets at the entrance gates in Tokyo as well as provincial tournaments and tours.

Each month the master and coaches of a stable receive their salaries from the sumo association, and the master receives additional payments for the feeding and training of his wrestlers and for the upkeep of the stable building and the practice rooms. The training fees are fixed, but the other payments are on a scale. For each wrestler of makushita and lower rank, the stablemaster receives ¥45,000 per month. Every tournament, he also gets a special bonus for each wrestler. For wrestlers in the makushita division and below, for example, he receives ¥80,000 as a special tournament allowance for each wrestler in a Tokyo tournament and ¥65,000 for a regional tournament.

Stables and individual wrestlers also receive income directly from patrons and supporters, and this is extremely difficult to quantify. It is a rich field for tax inspectors, and there have been cases of a stablemaster's being accused of evading taxes on large sums. Sumo patrons are known as *tanimachi,* a term said to have come from the district of that name in Osaka, where there once lived a physician who treated wrestlers for no fee. As this doctor's benevolence became common knowledge, the phrase "Tanimachi fan" was used to refer generally to a sumo enthusiast who contributed to the needs of professional wrestlers. The patronage system, however, dates back centuries earlier than the generous doctor. As popular literary and artistic genres made the champion wrestler into an urban hero, the merchants of Edo and Osaka in the middle and late Edo period formed the earliest sumo fan clubs. Among certain mercantile circles, treating a wrestler and his apprentices to lavish meals and outings was considered the greatest of extravagances. Being seen in the company of a wrestler was, and for that matter still is, an indication of wealth and status.

Today, patron organizations, known as *koenkai*, sponsor an individual wrestler or a whole stable. Those fan clubs supporting one man are likely to have a core of supporters from the stable's main patron club. They vary in size, depending on the rank and popularity of the wrestler. A club usually contributes financial aid to pay for elder stock when its wrestler retires. Most wrestlers will also be sponsored by patron organizations formed in their home town or region; a wrestler's first decorated apron for tournament ceremonies traditionally comes from his hometown sponsors. Patron organizations for stables are usually headed by powerful business leaders or politicians. Membership in these is sometimes restricted and elitist, and annual fees can range from a few thousand to tens of thousands of yen. When one of the stable's wrestlers advances to one of the upper ranks, the club customarily presents him with an expensive decorated apron, kesho mawashi, and a crested kimono. The patron organizations also award gifts of cash to those wrestlers who have finished a tournament with more wins than losses; and when a referee attached to the stable is promoted to the next rank, he will receive a new costume from the club. In addition to the koenkai organizations for the stable and for individual sekitori wrestlers, there are many informal groups which may entertain at modest expense junior wrestlers of promise or which may contribute moral rather than material support to sumo in general. Annual membership fees for such clubs are negligible, and they attract considerable student support. Other types of patron organizations also exist, such as the Tamari Kai in Tokyo and the Tozai Kai in Osaka. The members of such groups attend tournaments en masse and may occupy whole blocks of seats around the ring.

From Apprentice to Yokozuna   The objective of each stablemaster, needless to say, is to produce wrestlers of makuuchi caliber. Aside from the personal satisfaction involved, the master's status within the sumo association rises at the same time, and a stable with a number of high-ranking wrestlers tends to attract influential and wealthy patrons.

Recruiting new wrestlers became a difficult job in the recent period of prosperity, although in the early 1980s an upswing was seen. At one time the guarantee of free housing and a full belly was sufficient to lure droves of apprentices, but today, in an industrialized and affluent Japan, the financial uncertainty of professional sumo—only those in the juryo and makuuchi divisions receive a monthly salary, which means only some sixty-two out of over seven hundred wrestlers—has made it increasingly hard to find recruits. Not only is there no initial salary involved, but a boy entering a stable at the age of fifteen or sixteen faces long years of harsh discipline and hard work before he can even hope to reach one of the top ranks. An occasional college champion, such as Yutakayama, Wajima, or Asashio, advances to the makuuchi ranks in record time, but these are the exceptions. (In any case, a college champion is permitted to omit the lowest three divisions and start his professional career at the bottom of the makushita division.) Statistically, the chances of achieving yokozuna rank are slim enough to be daunting. This means that most wrestlers retire from professional sumo without ever having seen a monthly pay envelope. Such statistics are not lost on the parents of prospective wrestlers, and while the great success and popularity of the television-era champions may inspire many a largish Japanese youth to follow in their footsteps, friends and relatives usually try hard to dissuade these young hopefuls.

While not nearly as manifest as in professional baseball, sumo in recent years has developed an intensive scouting system. The largest stables, including Dewanoumi, Takasago, Tatsunami, and Sadogatake, have established scout networks throughout the country with the help of their nationwide patron organizations. Retired wrestlers and patron-club members act as part-time scouts for a stable, and acquaintances of the master or one of the stable's wrestlers often bring potential apprentices to the stablemaster's attention. When on provincial tours, masters are always on the lookout for potential talent and will use any means available to find it. The founder of Hanakago stable, for example, which was established in 1953 as an offshoot of the Nishonoseki stable, had formerly wrestled in amateur sumo groups, and much of his personal success in recruiting new wrestlers came as a direct result of the close connections he had maintained with the national amateur sumo organizations. On the other hand, popular and famous former champions, such as Taiho (Taiho stable), Tochinishiki (Kasugano), and Wakanohana (Futagoyama), have been able to attract youths very largely on the strength of their names.

Establishing a master-apprentice relationship with one of the stables does not automatically insure that a boy will be officially recognized as an apprentice by the sumo association. A potential professional wrestler must first satisfy the national compulsory education requirements by finishing junior high school. Occasionally a boy judged to have great potential will begin to train in a stable before completing that requirement, but he will continue to attend a school.

Young wrestlers up to eighteen must weigh at least 154 pounds and stand five feet seven inches (70 kilograms and 170 centimeters). Those nineteen and over must weigh 165 pounds and be over five feet eight inches in height (75 kilograms and 173 centimeters). However, to assure a boy's joining a stable, he may be accepted even if he is too light or too short, on the assumption that he will grow. No monetary allowance is made to a stable from the sumo association for training these youths until they are formally recognized as apprentices.

In former days the height and weight requirements for entering professional sumo were relatively loose, and it was sometimes possible to see a makunouchi wrestler who was less than five and a half feet tall. After World War II, however, in the face of scarcity of food combined with the steady increase in sumo's popularity, youths wishing to join the ranks of professional wrestlers inundated the stables, and with this greater choice, entrance requirements were gradually tightened up. In May 1957 a minimum weight of 174 pounds (79 kilograms) and a minimum height of five feet seven inches were established for aspirants under twenty-one, and 183 pounds (83 kilograms) and five feet eight inches for those over twenty-one. Even for the postwar generation, however, these standards proved to be a little high, and they were revised downward again to their present levels in 1969.

The physical examinations for acceptance as sumo apprentices are held just before each of the six annual tournaments under the supervision of elders appointed by the sumo association. There is little an aspirant can do to improve his height—though the former ozeki Asahikuni (now Oshima oyakata) recalls that he got a friend to hit him on the head with a billet of wood until it raised a lump of sufficient size—but for those who are somewhat under the weight requirement, there is a traditional technique for cheating the scale that even today is not unknown: the boy stuffs himself with sweet potatoes and drinks as much water as his stomach will hold, just before the weighing-in. The elders conducting the examination, however, are well aware of this ruse, having been through the same examination themselves. If a boy fails to meet the requirements, he must wait for the next time. There may, on rare occasions, be exceptions to this rule, but only with the approval of the directors of the sumo association, and then only if they judge that the boy will soon grow to meet the standards.

Once he passes the physical examination and his stablemaster has submitted documents of parental consent and a copy of his family register, the boy is officially an apprentice wrestler and as such belongs to the sumo association. Foreigners must also submit the signed (or sealed) statements of two reliable guarantors.

Once accepted, all apprentices must attend the training school run by the association. In the morning sessions, coaches conduct training in the basic techniques, such as *tsuriashi* (sliding the feet along the ground), *tachiai* (initial charge), and how to fall safely. From about ten-thirty or eleven they receive instruction in physiology, sports-related medicine, sumo history, and necessary accomplishments for the wrestler. During this time the apprentices remain in Tokyo and do not participate in any provincial tours, although they do take part in the main tournaments. Three times a year, following each of the Tokyo tournaments, there are school ceremonies at which prizes are awarded to outstanding students.

Passing the requirements and being entered on the official rolls of the association does not mean that the wrestler's name will appear on the ranking list. Except for collegiate champions, who are placed at the bottom of the makushita division, the new entrant begins in the maezumo class in the tournament immediately following his acceptance. The maezumo system was begun in the Edo period, although it was discontinued briefly between 1946 and 1956. In former times when there were very large numbers of aspirants, maezumo matches started very early in the morning on all days except the first and last. The youngsters, divided into east and west groups, waited seated on either side of the ring. The referee, also a youngster of the lowest rank, was undergoing his own apprenticeship. There was, in the old days, no warming-up period or delay of any kind. The two boys faced each other, clapped their hands, and charged with great energy in what was known as *tobitsuki*. The winner remained to face another opponent.

These days, however, smaller numbers, more annual tournaments, and a shorter average apprenticeship have led to maezumo contests that differ hardly at all from the regular bouts, which they immediately precede at the start of the day's schedule. The apprentice needs four wins to succeed, and if he gets them, then on the eighth day he and his fellows are presented to the general public at a mid-afternoon ceremony called the *shinjo shusse hiro*. Dressed in decorative aprons borrowed from seniors in their stables, the boys line up in rows, squatting to face the front. As their stables and names are called out, each one rises and executes a stiff bow. A junior referee, raising a folding fan borrowed from an announcer, announces their new status, after which the whole group rises and bows to front, east, rear, west, and again front, to be met with a wave of generous applause from each side in turn. This done, the boys are led away by the front west aisle—the only time this is used by wrestlers—and taken to pay their respects to the directors, referees, and other officials. Their sumo career has now begun, and they will be listed for the first time on the banzuke of the next tournament.

The only exception to this practice is the March tournament held in Osaka, when at the end of the school year, aspirants are numerous enough to require something closer to the old system. They still need their four wins, so a loser may have several attempts on the same day; and there are shinjo shusse ceremonies on the fifth, eighth, and thirteenth days. Naturally, the most skillful boys achieve their goal first; lately, the third presentation ceremony has even had a few boys who failed to get their four wins. As was said before, however, in other places and at other times the maezumo bouts are much the same as those of the jonokuchi. The sole difference is that only the wrestler's name, not his birthplace and stable, is called. For safety reasons, the tobitsuki jump-off was stopped and the boys had to first touch both hands to the ground—a requirement that in September 1984 was experimentally extended to all ranks, right to the very top.

Before World War II, when there were large numbers of new wrestlers, only three wins were required to advance to jonokuchi; but with only two tournaments a year, a large percentage of the aspirants, including the great Futabayama, had to wait two years or more before their names appeared on the *banzuke hyo,* the ranking list which is released by the sumo association thirteen days before a tournament. Historically, it served as a program, but in these days of long tournaments, this function has been taken over by a daily-issued printed list of bouts called the *torikumi hyo*. The banzuke, printed on large sheets of thin white paper and selling for a remarkably low price, is sent out to members of supporters' clubs and sold at the tournaments, but often is sold out rapidly. An annual order may be placed with the sumo association, which includes a handsome calendar in a package deal.

The banzuke is written in an old style of calligraphy similar to that developed in the late seventeenth or early eighteenth century for use in advertisements for the Kabuki theater. When the first Edo paper programs were printed with wood blocks in 1757, the lettering was done by the printer Mikawa Jiemon, who later became a sumo elder and took on the hereditary name of Negishi. Thus the peculiar style of writing he developed for use in sumo programs came to be known as *Negishi-ryu,* or Negishi style. The calligraphy used today was originated by one in the line of his successors, Negishi Kenkichi, around 1903. Since 1926, however, the banzuke lettering has been done by referees. Starting with the names of the titleholders and the makuuchi wrestlers at the top of the sheet, both the ranking and the size of the lettering diminish as one reads downward. When there is an odd number of wrestlers in a top rank, the additional name is listed as *haridashi,* or overhanging, and is added on an outcropping at the extreme left or right of the appropriate row. For each tournament, all the wrestlers are divided into eastern and western sides. The wrestlers of the east are listed on the right-hand half of the banzuke and those of the west, on the left.

The east-west division ceased to have competitive significance in 1947, but it enables at-a-glance comparisons to be made. The yokozuna with the best record in the preceding tournament heads the east side, the yokozuna rated second heads the west, and so on down the entire list, alternating names between east and west. Every wrestler below the status of ozeki is subject to a new ranking for each tournament. A man who wins more than half his matches, a situation known as *kachikoshi,* will retain his position or be promoted, while one who wins less than half, called *makekoshi,* is likely to be demoted unless those directly above and below him have even worse scores. At the top of a narrow column running down the center of the sheet are two large black characters reading *gomen komuru,* or permit granted, a holdover from the years between 1784 and 1868 when public performances of sumo required the sanction of the Edo authorities. Beneath this is a list of the referees, also in descending order of rank, and below that, the names of the judges in chronological order of appointment. In the fifth (and bottom) row of the sheet, in addition to the almost microscopic names of the jonokuchi wrestlers, are listed the names of the directors and other elders of the sumo association, except those already listed as judges. In the bottom left-hand corner bold characters read: "May it continue to draw full audiences yet another thousand and ten thousand years."

The young man's wrestling name makes its first appearance on the ranking list published for the tournament which follows his promotion out of maezumo. Granted, it is in the very bottom row, and done in characters so small that they are popularly known as *mushi megane:* needing a magnifying glass. But this initial appearance on the banzuke is the first major step in a wrestler's career, no matter how insignificant the print may seem. Above each wrestler's name is his native prefecture, or more strictly, the place where his family register is kept; and if he has just adopted a new wrestling name, the old one is written in small characters in the space between the prefecture and the new name.

A wrestler's success in the major tournaments determines the speed with which he advances up through the higher ranks. When there were only two tournaments each year, it was normal for a man to take seven years or more to go from jonokuchi to makuuchi status, although there were outstanding exceptions. Tochigiyama, who later became the master of the Kasugano stable, began in May 1911 at the top of the jonokuchi rank. After defeating all his opponents, he advanced in the following tournament to a position in the upper ranks of the jonidan division. Again he won all of his matches and was promoted in the summer of 1912 to sandamme status. Once more undefeated, he moved up to the makushita class in the winter, where he lost one match and was forced to remain in the makushita rank for another tournament. In the following winter matches, however, he was promoted to juryo status. After only three tournaments as a juryo wrestler, he entered the makuuchi division. This was in early 1915, just four years after he started. In 1917 he was promoted to ozeki status and, after two undefeated championships in that position, was recommended for promotion to yokozuna. Today, with six tournaments each year instead of only two, advancement for an outstanding wrestler can be considerably faster, although the average length of time required to reach the makuuchi division (assuming that it is reached at all) is still five to six years.

Jonokuchi, jonidan, sandamme, and makushita wrestlers appear for only seven of a tournament's fifteen days. The junior bouts average some thirty-six an hour for the first two or three hours of the day's sumo, so it will be seen that there is little time for cere-

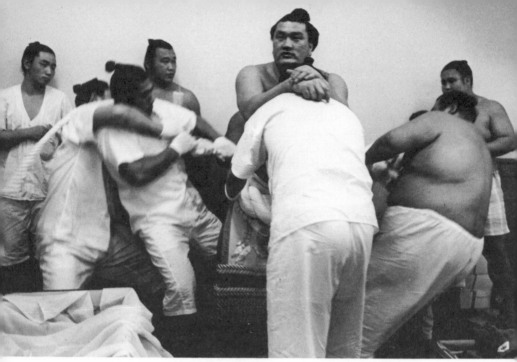

56. Wajima being helped with his yokozuna rope.

mony. No salt is thrown. It sometimes happens that the last few
wrestlers of the makushita division throw salt as if they were juryo
status, but there is no ritual significance in this; it is simply a device
to slow down the proceedings if there is too much time left before
the announced time of the juryo ring-entering ceremony.

The increasing intensity of competition as one moves up the ranks
forces many to drop out of professional sumo. The advance from
makushita to juryo is one of the most difficult. The maximum number of wrestlers in the juryo class is twenty-six, and no matter how
good a makushita wrestler's record may be, if a juryo wrestler
is not demoted, the makushita man cannot advance in rank. The
status difference between these two ranks is tremendous. Once a
man enters the juryo, he finally sheds the duties of a junior wrestler
and is called a sekitori. Now he is in a position to be served by the
lower-ranked wrestlers. He is given a wickerwork trunk (*akeni*)
lacquered green and red, his name painted on it, in which to store
the decorated aprons and silk belts used during a tournament. He is
permitted to have a fan club, and to have cotton material with
his name printed on it to give out as souvenir lengths to make
yukata, the summer kimono. He is permitted to wear on formal
occasions the formal kimono with haori and hakama. He joins in

the ring-entering ceremony of his own rank and wrestles on every day of a tournament. He has assigned to him his own tsukebito, a junior of his own stable who will henceforth wait on him and run his errands. And for the first time, he will receive a monthly salary instead of the meager *basho teate*, the tournament allowance that is all the non-sekitori get.

Even more difficult an achievement than the jump to juryo is the advancement from that rank to makuuchi status, although exceptionally skilled wrestlers have been known to do this in two tournaments. The usual number of makuuchi wrestlers below titleholders is twenty-six, and their position is graded according to their last performance. In general, a makuuchi wrestler moves up one step for every win over seven that he gains in a tournament, though much depends on the scores of those ranked above and below him. The same proviso applies to the sanyaku ranks of komusubi and sekiwake, but generally, having more losses than wins means almost certain demotion. The ozeki rank, however, carries certain privileges. An ozeki will not be demoted unless he suffers more losses than wins in *two* successive tournaments, and even if this should happen, he will be restored to the ozeki rank if he shows a good performance—ten wins at least—in the tournament following his demotion. To attain ozeki rank, a man must have wrestled as a sekiwake in three successive tournaments with more wins than losses, and with a total of at least thirty-two wins— though if an ozeki is thought to be needed, the rules may be bent a little. Also required is the recommendation of the board of directors of the sumo association. A formal announcement is then made at the new ozeki's stable, followed by a short ceremony.

According to the regulations of the yokozuna review committee, created in 1951, a wrestler must either win two successive tournaments as an ozeki or have shown "equivalent success" in order to gain the yokozuna rank. Very few men indeed are able to qualify for the yokozuna position by fulfilling the first requirement. Only Futabayama, Tochinishiki, Taiho, Kitanofuji, and Koto-zakura in the last fifty years have been able to win two tournaments in a row as ozeki. The committee also stresses the need for strength of character, for a yokozuna should represent all that is best in sumo. In May 1978, in recommending Wakamisugi for the rank of yokozuna, the committee attached a statement that he "should behave in a manner befitting a children's idol and not keep darting glances about."

The name of a wrestler who, in the sumo association's eyes, meets the requirements for yokozuna is submitted to the review committee, which confers on the second day following the end of the tournament. If it unanimously approves the choice, the advancement is made official the next day. As with the selection of a new ozeki, representatives of the association are sent to the wrestler's stable to inform him and his master, and a ritual takes place to confer the yokozuna title. A message is also sent to the descendant of the Yoshida family in Kumamoto. In the stable itself, preparations are immediately begun for the making of the new yokozuna's first ceremonial *tsuna*, the white rope-like belt that is his symbol and, in its compound form *-zuna*, gives him the second half of his title. The making of it is a vigorous ritual known as the *tsunauchi shiki*, a ceremony that takes place every time a clean rope is needed, before the Tokyo tournaments. The training area is covered with white canvas. All the wrestlers of that stable and related ones undergo a purification ritual. They wear their cotton practice belts, dark or white according to their rank, which they cover with white towels to keep the rope clean. They wear white cotton gloves for the same reason. On their heads they wear the *hachimaki*, the rolled sweatband of the working Japanese, but this time in auspicious red and white. Three lengths of white cotton are laid on the canvas. Hemp, beaten in rice bran until soft, is spread along them. Copper wires are added as stiff cores, and the cotton is rolled up sideways to form three long sausages bulkier in the middle than at the ends. The smooth wooden pillar used for teppo practice has meanwhile been covered with padding, and the three strands of cotton rope are looped around it. To the sound of a drum, two groups of wrestlers begin to pull from the ends, twisting the strands together in short bursts of furious activity. To ensure the even distribution of the twisted coils, another wrestler, a white cloth over his head to protect the rope from his hair oil, sits in front of the pillar underneath the rope, and hangs his weight from it. The weight of the finished rope varies, but they often reach over thirty pounds.

As soon as the rope is finished, the new grand champion and his two attendants dress up in borrowed ceremonial aprons and are joined by a senior referee. An experienced yokozuna then gives instruction in the yokozuna version of the *dohyo iri*, the ring-entering ceremony. Once the ring-entering ceremony is mastered, the new yokozuna takes part in an installation ritual held at the Meiji Shrine in Tokyo. This always takes place in the middle of the morning on the Saturday immediately following the tournament in which the man qualified for yokozuna status. At the shrine, the wrestler receives his official documents of rank from the head of the sumo association, and following a ritual purification of his new rope, he goes out into the courtyard and performs his first public ring-entering ceremony—again, in borrowed finery, for there has not been time to have his own set of three embroidered aprons made.

A yokozuna is never demoted; the rank is his till he retires. If he has a run of losses, however, he usually drops out in mid-tournament, and if his record in successive tournaments is bad enough, pressure is usually placed on him to retire.

Wages A monthly wage system for professional wrestlers was begun in May 1957, but only sekitori wrestlers receive such salaries. Wrestlers below juryo rank are given no monthly wages, although each tournament they receive the allowance called basho teate: makushita wrestlers receive ¥80,000; sandamme, ¥70,000; jonidan, ¥65,000; and jonokuchi, ¥60,000. As of January 1985, the basic salary of a yokozuna was ¥812,000, while an ozeki received ¥675,000; a sekiwake or komusubi got ¥518,000, a maegashira ¥428,000, and a juryo, ¥364,000. In addition to these basic sums there are many other allowances and bonuses, making it well-nigh impossible for an outsider to compute the actual income of a specific wrestler: a supplementary allowance of ¥25,000, paid to all sekitori after every Tokyo tournament; bonuses for top-rankers, ¥200,000 for a yokozuna, ¥150,000 for an ozeki, and ¥50,000 for a sekiwake or a komusubi; additional tournament allowances, also varying according to rank, and, for the Tokyo tournaments, ¥150,000 to each yokozuna for the renewal of his yokozuna rope.

In addition, championship (yusho) prize moneys are set for each division. The makuuchi championship—*the* championship—brings a ¥2,000,000 cash reward. The winning juryo wrestler receives ¥550,000, the makushita champion, ¥250,000, the winners of the sandamme and jonidan divisions, ¥100,000, and of the jonokuchi, ¥50,000. In the top division, the three special prizes—fighting spirit, technique, and outstanding performance—are worth ¥550,000 each.

Wages and allowances are linked to a man's performance only as far as it affects his rank. A drop or rise in rank will mean a corresponding change in salary and bonuses.

Before the establishment of the monthly pay system, the only financial reward received directly by a wrestler was the "accumulated money"—*mochi kyukin,* or *hoshokin* (incentive pay), as it is officially called. This is computed for every wrestler after each tournament, beginning with the passage from maezumo, but nothing is paid on the figure until the wrestler reaches juryo status.

It is primarily based on the number of wins over losses the man records in his career. A beginner starts with a credit of three yen. For each victory over the half-mark, the basic sum is raised by fifty sen—half a yen—though nothing is taken away if he has more losses than wins. Promotion to juryo status raises the figure to forty yen, in case the wrestler has not accumulated that amount, and it is at this level that the man begins to get extra pay based on the figure. Promotion to makuuchi ensures a minimum figure of sixty yen, to ozeki one hundred yen, and to yokozuna one hundred and fifty yen. A maegashira who beats a yokozuna is awarded a *kimboshi* (gold star) which adds another ten yen to his basic sum. The top-division championship is worth a thirty-yen addition, or fifty yen if the winner is undefeated. With the exception of the promotion additions, which are lost by demotion, the accumulated figure is always added to and never subtracted from. When a wrestler suffers more losses than wins, there is simply no addition to his basic amount, although gold star increments are always added regardless of the rest of the man's performance.

The basic figure is used like this: following every tournament, each wrestler over the makushita rank is paid 1,500 times the sum he has accumulated. This can run to incredible amounts. While in September 1970 the yokozuna Kitanofuji had accumulated 324.5 yen-points, the then komusubi Takanohana, 68, and the third maegashira Takamiyama, 90, the yokozuna Taiho had a total of 1,442 yen-points. (At his retirement, Takamiyama had still only advanced to a total of 266.5.) At that time Taiho had won the championship thirty-one times, eight of these undefeated. Just for the championships, his basic figure was increased by ¥1,090. The fifty sen he received for each of his kachikoshi wins from his first matches in the jonokuchi division in 1956 brought his total in September 1970 to the ¥1,442 figure. In those days the basic sum was multiplied by 1,000, so he received after that tournament nearly ¥1,500,000 in hoshokin, which, when added to his monthly salary and other bonuses, brought him a considerable income by any account.

The rewards, then, for a successful wrestler are not limited to exposure on television or a few meals on patrons' accounts. The financial gains can be great; in that possibility, together with the extremely high status awarded to wrestlers in Japanese society today, lies sumo's greatest attraction to aspiring wrestlers. Those who manage to find the legendary "treasure in the ring," however, are few: only one out of ten wrestlers ever receives any pay, aside from tournament allowances, during his professional career.

Wrestling Names The names under which sumo wrestlers fight, whether their legal names or professional ones, are called shikona. The earliest wrestling names appeared during the feudal warring period (mid-fifteenth to mid-sixteenth century), when destitute masterless samurai, forced to rely on their skill as wrestlers to make a living, were ashamed to use their real names. Instead they adopted the names of their birthplaces or of famous rivers or mountains. Not long afterward, other wrestlers began to use the device of the wrestling name to make a favorable impression on their audiences. Fierce-sounding titles such as Ikazuchi (Thunder), Inazuma (Lightning), and Oarashi (Great Storm) appeared in the literature of the sixteenth century. The tendency to use characters meaning animals, weapons, gods, and the harsher of the natural phenomena in a name in order to strengthen the wrestler's image grew tremendously during the early Edo period; the term shikona, in fact, was originally written with the characters meaning "strong name." Names such as Nio (Guardian King), Onikatsu (Devil Beater), Yamaoroshi (Wind Blowing Down from the Mountain Peaks), and Shishigatake (Lion Peak) were common. Wrestling names of the late eighteenth and early nineteenth centuries—Tanikaze (Valley Wind), Raiden (Thunder and Lightning), Kimenzan (Mountain with a Devil's Face), and Arauma (Wild Horse)—were in that tradition.

In modern times, many wrestlers have taken place names from the regions where they were born. Kurohimeyama, for instance, was named after a mountain in Niigata, and Washuyama from one in Okayama. Aobayama and Aobajo took their names from a mountain and castle in Miyagi Prefecture. Kitanoumi (Northern Sea) is a reference to Hokkaido and Mienoumi (Sea of Mie) came from that yokozuna's home prefecture of Mie.

Some wrestlers borrow part of their new names from that of someone who has been important in their lives or careers. The wrestler Maedayama active in the 1930s and 1940s was such a case. After successfully recovering from a serious accident, he showed his gratitude to the physician who had operated on him, Dr. Maeda Wasaburo, by taking the doctor's family name and adding -*yama,* meaning mountain, to it.

A very common practice is for the stablemaster to give his wrestlers a name incorporating a character from his own shikona, that of one of his predecessors, or from the stable's name. There has been an entire string of wrestlers using the character *tochi* (horse chestnut) in honor of Tochigiyama, the eighth master of the Kasugano stable: Tochinishiki, Tochinoumi, Tochihikari, Tochiisami, and so on. The *dewa* of the Dewanoumi stable and the *sada* of the current master's shikona Sadanoyama are likewise frequently found in wrestling names of that stable. The most notable example is the Sadogatake stable, whose master is the former Kotozakura. All the members of this stable have names beginning with *Koto* (a zitherlike instrument).

Some stables have special names that are considered to belong to them. The Takasago stable usually awards the name Asashio to a wrestler only after he has made the sanyaku grade, although the collegiate champion Nagaoka was given it in early 1979 as a mae-gashira wrestler. In the Tatsunami stable, the name Haguroyama is given only to the chosen successor to the stablemaster. Since the early nineteenth century the Isenoumi stable has handed down the name Kashiwado to its best men. The Nishonoseki stable has its own tradition in the name of Kaizan Taro, which was the original fighting name of the Meiji-era wrestler Tomozuna, who founded the Tomozuna stable after his retirement. One of his protégés, who took the name Kaizan Taro for luck, became the master of Nishonoseki stable after his own retirement, and the name became a tradition in that stable. The famous sumo broadcaster Kamikaze also had the name during World War II, as did, later, the wrestler Daitenryu.

Today, many wrestlers appear under their own names, at least for a while. In the late 1930s it became a tradition in the Dewanoumi stable for wrestlers to use their legal names until they reached the makushita class. Only those with names common to other wrestlers would have a different shikona, often made by prefixing *O-*(great) or appending -yama (mountain) to their real name, for it is a rule that no two men may have the same name on the ranking list. The trend has extended to many of the other stables, and some wrestlers have made it as far as juryo or even makuuchi class under their own names; the great yokozuna Wajima never changed his name at all. Recently, however, the sumo association condemned this tendency and as a result far more special fighting names have been seen since the late 1970s. A foreigner entering sumo must have a Japanese shikona from the beginning, since he needs a name which can be written in Chinese characters.

Wrestling names tend to follow patterns, and various names and characters have fallen into disuse, either because of changed social conditions or out of superstition. During the 1920s and 1930s, the suffix *-takè*, which means mountain peak, was extremely popular. After a number of wrestlers using that character in their names suddenly suffered losses and unexpected setbacks in the ring, however, the ending came to be avoided. Recent years have seen it coming back, but it is still not common. During the years of westernization and cultural confusion following the Meiji Restoration, a number of odd names appeared on the scene, including Denkito (Electric Light Bulb), Kikaisen (Mechanical Boat), Kataokame (One-eyed Mask of a Fat Woman), and Togarashi (Red Pepper). The wars with China and Russia in the 1890s and 1900s brought on such names as Nihonkai (Japan Sea), Taiho (Cannon, written with different characters from the name of the great yokozuna Taiho), and Oryokko (Yalu River). During the Pacific War, however, wrestling names that reflected the war were not popular. And when the country's fortunes took a turn for the worse and the casualties of the famous kamikaze airplane squads mounted, the wrestler Kamikaze (whose name actually means divine wind, a phrase commemorating the great storm that kept the Mongols from invading Japan in the thirteenth century) was asked to change his name.

Wrestling names remain a vibrant and eloquent part of the sumo tradition, not least because they are so tied up with luck. All sports and other risky occupations have their superstitions, but none more so than sumo. A man who is having a run of bad luck, or one who wants a little extra impetus, is likely to change his name. Sometimes the change is radical, sometimes only one character is altered to another of the same sound (the -shio of Asashio has been varied, for instance). When the ozeki Takanohana was making a strong bid for yokozuna, he changed the no of his name to the more old-fashioned form that had been used by his elder brother when he was the yokozuna Wakanohana I. When the bid failed, he returned to his former way of writing it. The custom makes it rather difficult to follow the careers of some men who have made several attempts to avert ill fortune or attract good. This custom is by no means uncommon among ordinary Japanese, but it is at its most flamboyant in the world of sumo.

6. Organization and Tournaments

Kokugikan Tournaments held in Tokyo take place at the Kokugikan, the national sumo stadium. This is the only hall devoted to sumo: the Osaka, Nagoya and Fukuoka tournaments are staged in gymnasiums which have their seating modified for each occasion, while provincial tours, usually consisting of one-day stands, utilize halls or, frequently, are held out-of-doors. A number of buildings have held the name Kokugikan, which means hall of the kokugi—national sport. For the space of a week or so in early May 1983, three Kokugikans existed together, in a manner of speaking: the old Kokugikan in Ryogoku had been demolished but its rubble had not yet been carted away; the Kuramae Kokugikan was busy with preparations for the May tournament; and the foundations of the new Kokugikan, midway between the two, were being laid.

The old Ryogoku Kokugikan, which had opened in June 1909 and been rebuilt after a fire in 1917, was heavily damaged in the Second World War and was subsequently taken over by the Occupation forces. This led to the sumo association's decision to build a new hall on the Tokyo side of the Sumida River, half a mile upstream. From its opening in September 1954 to its last tournament in September 1984, the Kuramae Kokugikan was the heart of professional sumo. Not far away is a small shrine, the Kuramae Hachiman, all that remains of the once-great religious complex where the first Edo-period sumo programs printed on paper were issued, in 1757. Most of the land occupied by the complex was gradually sold off by the early decades of the twentieth century, but a large lot was later secured by the sumo association as the site of the Kuramae stadium.

Eventually, the association decided for a number of reasons that it was better to build a new, modern hall rather than try to refurbish the shabby one at Kuramae, and secured a plot just north of Ryogoku station. Work began in the spring of 1983, with an opening date set for January 1985. The system would not be noticeably changed, but the new building was designed to incorporate modern techniques and bring sumo into the electronic age.

Outside the main entrance gates to the Kokugikan were twenty catering stalls. One of many holdovers from the feudal period, these so-called teahouses, chaya, are allocated entire blocks of the best seats in the hall, which they in turn sell to regular patrons. Tickets for good box seats, known as *sajiki* or *masuseki,* are almost impossible to obtain without connections with one of the businesses or government offices that monopolize them for each tournament. The price of a seat in one of the four-person box seats comes to about ¥15,000 if refreshments, sakè or beer, and souvenirs are included. Teahouse attendants, known as *dekata,* many of whom are farmers from outside Tokyo and serve year after year in the Tokyo tournaments, hurry about the hall during the matches, guiding their patrons to seats and keeping them supplied with food and drink. Many of the dekata also serve at Osaka and Nagoya.

Four narrow aisles lead down through the crowded rows of box seats that cover the main floor up to the wrestling platform in the center of the stadium. The two aisles used by the eastern and western wrestlers to enter the hall are known as *hanamichi,* or "flower paths." The term dates to the Heian period, when the "left" wrestlers wore hollyhock flowers in their hair as they entered the courtyard at the imperial palace from the east to perform before the emperor, and the "right" wrestlers wore calabash blossoms as they approached from the west. When sumo was performed before the present emperor at the imperial palace in pre-World War II Tokyo, the two aisles that the wrestlers used were decorated with cherry blossoms and chrysanthemums (the imperial symbol), and flowers were given to the winning wrestlers. The hanamichi found in the Kabuki theater is of a different origin.

Between the foremost box seats and the wrestling platform

57. *The inside of the new Kokugikan at Ryogoku. The banners above the roof give thanks for a capacity audience—which there was every day of the January*

1985 tournament, a record in recent sumo history. Portraits of tournament winners hang over the balconies.

are six rows of cushions known as *sunakaburi*, or sand-covered seats, a term easily understood if one has ever seen a wrestler go flying out of the ring, which is covered with sand, and into the spectators who are sitting on these cushions. The boxes, which usually contain four cushions, extend from the sunakaburi to the back of the hall and are separated from each other by low-lying steel bars. In former times they were delineated by hemp ropes and seated up to eight persons. At that time, too, they had matting floors, later replaced with plain wood and carpeting. Balconies on the second floor of Kuramae Kokugikan were converted to western-style tip-up seats in the late 1950s, with extremely inexpensive wooden benches at the very top reaching nearly to the ceiling. Tickets are labeled *shomen* (main side), *muko-jomen* (opposite side), *higashi-gawa* (eastern side), and *nishi-gawa* (western side). Traditionally the Japanese emperor has always sat facing south, and seen from that perspective—the "main side"—everything on his left was to the east, and on his right, to the west. Logistics dictated that when the Kuramae Kokugikan was built, the main side, toward which all the action was directed, had to be set on the southern side of the building instead of the northern, so that the "east" of the stadium was actually on the western side of the hall, and "west" on the eastern. This arbitrary orientation for sumo happens in any place where convenience counts more than compass direction.

In the case of the new Ryogoku Kokugikan, the orientation is east-west; that is, the main side fronts on the road that runs parallel with the Sumida River; thus the "east" side is actually north. This splendid building, officially opened with the January tournament of 1985, has for the first time incorporated all the scattered facilities into one master plan. The sumo school for beginners is located at the rear on the second floor, and the clinic has been moved from small premises in nearby Chitose to the first basement, where there are also committee rooms and storerooms for archives and other museum property. The second basement is mainly parking facilities, but patrons are still strongly advised to travel by train. The chaya mentioned earlier now have a position inside the main building, and are reached by the door to the left of the big main entrance. Other patrons enter by the main entrance, which, rather than being a corridor, is a large hall, with a wide display case for the trophies at the far end. The third entrance in the symmetrical facade is to the right, and has doors opening into the sumo museum and the sumo association offices.

The imposing front has massive granite staircases leading up on either side to the second-floor balcony, which overhangs half of the first-floor seating of the auditorium. This is, of necessity, basically the same as any other sumo hall, but has been planned to attract other events outside of tournament time. The ring can be automatically raised and lowered, the ringside seats dismantled, and the front rows of seats telescoped by computer control until they fit underneath the permanent seats at the rear of the first floor. The boxes are slightly larger than those of the old Kuramae Kokugikan, but the total capacity is much the same: about eleven thousand. Above the permanent boxes of the first floor there is a large balcony with tip-up cinema-type seats that are sold singly. There are also special boxes for the handicapped, with easy access for wheelchairs. The four sides are somewhat truncated, giving wider corner areas, in keeping with the shape of the whole building. The acoustics are noticeably better, and the whole auditorium has a feeling of light and space.

The Ring   In the very center of the hall is the dohyo, a two-foot-high, eighteen-foot-square mound of clay so tightly packed that to build a completely new one requires eight truckloads of earth. In the new Ryogoku Kokugikan, the whole thing can be raised and lowered so that the hall can be put to other uses. In use, the top surface of the platform is covered with a thin layer of sand, which is commonly used as a symbol of purity in Shinto rituals, but which has the added advantages of preventing slipping and assisting in judgments when a footprint can determine whether or not a wrestler stepped out of the ring. Small cylindrical rice-straw bales called *tawara,* filled with earth and tied tightly with straw rope, are sunk into the clay base to mark off an inner circle of approximately fifteen feet in diameter. One bale is left out in each of the four cardinal directions and a larger one placed outside to cover the gap; originally this was to allow for drainage of rainwater when tournaments were held outdoors. These four are called *toku-dawara,* or "privilege bales," because at these four points a step outside the normal circumference of the ring will not be considered a loss. More straw bales are used to outline the square edge of the mound and strengthen the steps cut in the side.

Suspended directly above the platform is the *tsuriyane,* a huge wooden roof of a style found in major Shinto shrines. From the end of the seventeenth century the roof was held up by four columns, but in 1932 these were removed because they obstructed the view. They were replaced by huge silk tassels hung from the corners of the roof and dyed the colors of the cloth that had formerly been wrapped round the pillars: green for spring, red for summer, white for autumn, and black for winter. Small tassels are also hung in the center of each side of the roof. Square baskets filled with salt are placed on the corners of the mound underneath the big red and white tassels, and, when the juryo bouts begin, cedar buckets filled with water are stood in niches dug into the corners. The salt and water are used in short purification rituals performed by juryo and makuuchi wrestlers.

Referees   Directing and refereeing the matches in professional sumo are the gyoji, whose duties include performing the rituals that take place before the tournaments—purifying the stadium and the ring—and overseeing the conduct of the matches. Referees of juryo rank and up wear heavy silk kimono of a type used by samurai during the Muromachi period and black court hats. Promotion for referees is very slow, since it goes largely by seniority, and it may be further delayed by a record of misjudgments. The highest rank is that of *tate gyoji*, or chief referee, and he and his deputy oversee only the last three matches. The chief referee always bears the hereditary name Kimura Shonosuke, and his deputy, that of Shikimori Inosuke.

Each referee carries a wooden war fan, with which he an-

58. Takanohana lifts Tamanofuji out of the ring with a tsuri dashi.

nounces the contestants, signals the time to begin the bout, indicates his decision, and proclaims the winner. His rank can be seen in the color of the tassel attached to the handle of his fan and in the cords and rosettes on his costume. The chief gyoji has purple, and his deputy, purple-and-white; referees of sanyaku rank have vermilion, and regular makuuchi ones have red-and-white. Juryo gyoji have green-and-white, and all those below that rank have green or, rarely, black. Referees of juryo rank and above have finer-quality fans, trimmed with silver or even gold and, often, lacquered. Lower-ranking referees, who in old times began their training as children and served an apprenticeship of several years before being allowed to referee in public, now begin at the same age, about sixteen, as the young wrestlers. They wear cotton costumes of much the same pattern as their seniors' but drawn up and tied below the knees. They are barefoot, whereas juryo and makuuchi referees wear tabi, split-toed white socks, and sanyaku and above also wear straw *zori* (sandals) even in the ring.

Every referee assumes the name of either Kimura or Shikimori, hereditary lines that emerged as the most powerful of the Edo-period referee families in the mid-eighteenth century. A viewer who watches closely can discern which line a referee belongs to by the way he grips his fan when announcing the wrestlers before a match: a Kimura keeps the back of his hand up, whereas a Shikimori has his thumb and fingers turned upward.

Apparel   The basic garment of sumo is the *mawashi*, a length of cloth about two-and-a-half feet wide and up to thirty-eight feet in length. The formal term for the costly silk belt is *torimawashi* or *shimekomi*. It is the key to many of the seventy-odd official techniques of sumo wrestling. It is folded lengthwise six times, wrapped around the groin and waist, and tied in a flat knot at the back. Its present form was developed in the late eighteenth century. In the ring, wrestlers of makushita rank and below wear the same dark-colored cotton belt they use for training, but add the sagari, the fringe of long twisted strings attached to a strip of cloth that is tucked into the front of the belt. There are usually nineteen strings, though the number varies between seventeen and twenty-one. Since they are patterned after the sacred ropes that hang down in front of Shinto shrines, which are always an uneven number, even numbers of sagari are never used. Outside of tournaments, sekitori too wear the cotton training belts, in their case white, but for public bouts they appear in a mawashi of silk or satin, formerly dark but now often dyed a vivid color to look well on television. The sagari are of the same color, and are stiffly starched so that they look like wires, unlike the loose strings of the junior ranks. The sagari have no function at all, and the strip often comes off in the course of a bout, when it is the referee's duty to toss it out of the ring to prevent it from getting underfoot.

Ring-Entering Ceremonies Matches, which begin about ten or eleven in the morning, are staged in ascending order of rank. Junior bouts take place with minimal ceremony in quick succession until mid-afternoon. The prematch rituals get more involved as the status of the contestants climbs. Throughout the day excitement builds, and the audience grows as increasingly higher-ranked men ascend the platform. For junior bouts only about one-third of the lights are used, and a thrill runs through the house as the remainder are turned on, usually for the juryo ring-entering ceremony, but earlier if there is a good crowd or the television crews want to capture an interesting bout. By three or three-thirty the house is filling up rapidly with customers who wish to see only the sekitori bouts from the expensive boxes. Sometime between three and four o'clock, the television crews begin their transmissions. Before the makuuchi wrestlers come on, if the tickets are completely sold out, four white

59. Wrestlers facing the crowd during the ring-entering ceremony. Facing camera, from left, are Kurosegawa, Yutakayama, and Takanosato.

banners bearing the characters *man' in onrei*, "full house, our thanks," descend electronically from the ceiling.

Just before the first of the sekitori matches, the wrestlers of juryo rank appear together for the dohyo iri, the ring-entering ceremony. On the first and subsequent odd-numbered days of the tournament those on the east side come on first; on even-numbered days the western side goes first. (The announcing of the contestants for each bout alternates similarly.) The wrestlers, wearing richly embroidered decorative aprons presented to them by their patron organizations, are preceded down the hanamichi and onto the platform by a referee of the same rank, who squats on his heels in the center of the ring, his fan held parallel to the ground. The wrestlers are introduced in ascending order of rank. As each man hears his name, birthplace, and stable announced on the public address system, he climbs up and walks round the ring to his place, and a circle is gradually formed facing outward toward the audience. As the last one mounts the platform, they all turn in, clap their hands, raise their right arms, lift up their aprons slightly with both hands, raise both arms briefly, and then turn and file out in the same order. The ritual is then repeated by the wrestlers of the other side. Later, when the juryo matches are over, the makuuchi wrestlers repeat the ceremony, after which all the yokozuna come on one by one and perform their own form of dohyo iri.

The brief ring-entering ceremony, which dates back to the late seventeenth or early eighteenth century, was at one time much more elaborate. During the Edo period the number of wrestlers was far smaller than it is today, and the high-ranking wrestlers entered the ring one by one to the sound of wooden clappers beaten by a referee (this is now done by an announcer). Once in the ring, they stamped their feet on the ground and clapped their hands together, much as the yokozuna do today. Beginning around the turn of this century, the number of maegashira and juryo wrestlers increased, and, in order to permit them all to perform a dohyo iri, the ceremony was changed to its present abbreviated form. The clapping of hands, also performed in front of Shinto shrines, indicates that the bodies and spirits of the wrestlers have been purified. Raising the arms shows that the wrestlers, who were once recruited from the ranks of the samurai, are not concealing any weapons, and lifting the aprons is meant to take the place of stamping the feet on the ground. The entire ceremony is supposed to signify a pledge to the deities that the wrestlers will fight fairly and with the proper spirit.

Following the last of the juryo matches and the ring-entering ceremony of the makuuchi wrestlers, the yokozuna enters the hall for his own dohyo iri. Over his decorated apron is the huge snow-white rope of his rank, tied in the back into a sweeping knot. Hanging down from the front are five of the zigzag folded paper strips, gohei, that are used in Shinto ritual. The yokozuna is led into the ring by the chief referee or his deputy and is accompanied by two maegashira wrestlers, one known as the *tsuyu harai* (dew-sweeper), who acts as a herald, and the other as the *tachi mochi* (sword-bearer), who carries the yokozuna's long curved sword in its scabbard upright in his right hand. If the yokozuna's own stable has no wrestlers of maegashira rank, these two assistants will be provided by another stable in the same ichimon, or group. The yokozuna ring-entering ceremony was first performed in 1789 by Tanikaze Kajinosuke in the days when wrestlers were usually retained by feudal lords. The yokozuna's juniors then carried the swords that attested to his samurai status.

Two styles of yokozuna ring-entering ceremonies are recognized today: the Unryu and the Shiranui, names given because they are supposed to reflect the majestic ways in which the ceremony was performed in the Edo period by Unryu Hisakichi and Shiranui Koemon. In fact, during the Meiji era the yokozuna all displayed quite individual forms of the dohyo iri, and it is impossible to label any of them Unryu or Shiranui. But when the yokozuna Haguro-yama imitated Tachiyama's style in 1931, someone decided that his was a form handed down from the great Shiranui, and so it was given that name. Another style favored at that time and based on the performance of Nishinoumi II was then labeled the Unryu style. The differences between the two styles are described below.

Whichever style the yokozuna follows, the three wrestlers first squat at the side from which they have entered. Flanked on either side by his attendants, the yokozuna brings his arms together in two resounding claps. Following each clap he rubs his hands together at arm's length before him and then brings them out horizontally with palms upward on either side of his body. This is known as *chiri o kiru* and comes from the samurai practice of purifying the hands and body by wiping them with grass before a battle. Leaving his attendants at the side of the ring, he stands up and strides to the center, turns to face the front (and the television cameras), and swings his arms out and together in another clap. He places his feet wide apart, and, with his left hand on his rib cage, extends his right out at the side. Reversing the position of his hands, he next raises his right leg as high as he possibly can and them brings the foot slamming down on the sand. The yokozuna brings himself slowly and dramatically upright by inching his feet

60. *Wajima performing the yokozuna dohyo iri. Misugiiso acts as sword-bearer and Arase as dew sweeper.*

forward. It is here that the two styles of dohyo iri part company, if only briefly: in the Unryu style, the yokozuna repeats the left-hand-on-rib-cage, right-arm-out movement; in the Shiranui style he lowers both hands out and down and brings them up slowly. The different traditions merge again as he repeats the stamping (shiko) twice more, alternating legs and pressing his hand down each time on his knee with all his might. Shiko is practiced by all wrestlers as a limbering-up exercise but was originally meant as the rather graphic expression of the intention to vanquish an opponent by trampling him down and grinding his skull into the ground. The stamping is also supposed to frighten away any malignant spirits. The yokozuna then turns, walks back to the side of the ring, and resumes his former squatting position between his two attendants, who have not moved a muscle in the meantime. He repeats the chiri o kiru, turns and climbs down from the platform, and with his attendants leaves the hall, followed by the chief referee, who has been squatting near the rear of the ring for the whole of the time. The ritual is repeated by all the yokozuna taking part in the tournament.

Makuuchi Matches　There are two dressing rooms (*shitaku-beya*) at the back of the Kokugikan. They have television sets so that the wrestlers can view the ongoing matches and study the techniques of their rivals. Temperaments vary, but many sekitori men lounge around in shorts, resting, reading, or playing Japanese chess (*shogi*) until they are notified by their attendants that it is nearing the time to go into the hall. Their attendants put on their silk belts for them, after which the wrestlers begin their warm-up exercises. A wrestler enters the hall two matches before his own, taking a seat on a large cushion on the appropriate side of the ring. As each man mounts the platform, his personalized cushion is carried out and replaced with that of the next-but-one wrestler. The dressing rooms themselves are labeled east and west, and each wrestler waits his turn on the side on which he will be competing, which is not necessarily the side on which he is listed on the banzuke ranking list.

Although on the banzuke the wrestlers are apparently divided into two teams, the officials are not bound to keep to this division when pairing up opponents for a match, especially in the later days of a tournament. They also ignore the relative size and weight of individual wrestlers when assigning opponents. The matches for each day, which are announced twenty-four hours in advance, are decided upon by sumo association officials and can never be questioned or changed. If a wrestler takes ill, he forfeits the bout arranged for that day. The wrestler normally enters the hall from the side on which he is listed, but if both men in a bout are listed on the same side, the man with the higher rank is always the one to enter from his officially-designated direction.

Unless time is short, a referee of at least sanyaku rank comes in and reads the pairings arranged for the next day. A short intermission follows before the matches of the makuuchi wrestlers commence. The announcer, yobidashi, dressed in a kimono that often bears a commercial advertisement on the back and is tucked into the tight leggings of the traditional working man, a garment called *tattsuke-bakama,* steps forward into the center of the ring. Extending a plain white folding fan which he slowly opens, he faces first one side and then the other, calling out the direction, east or west, and the names of the wrestlers, in a high-pitched, quavering voice. The basic tune used is the same, but each man has his own little ornaments which mark his performance. He retreats, and as the wrestlers ascend the platform to begin their warming-up exercises, they are announced once more by the referee, with a style of voice production akin to that used in Kabuki. Meanwhile other yobidashi climb up and parade satin banners before the audience to announce patrons who will be giving prize money to the winner of the match. This custom began in the late seventeenth century when wealthy merchants in Osaka and Kyoto started to offer monetary gifts to the victor; at that time the referee would announce their names and the amounts donated. Following World War II, when money was tight and goods were scarce, patrons donated items of food and clothing. In 1984 each banner represented ¥40,000: ¥20,000 is received in cash by the winner, ¥5,000 is kept by the sumo association for expenses, and the remaining ¥15,000 is placed in a special account reserved to pay the wrestler's income tax.

The two contestants go to their corners, perform shiko, and then receive a ladle of water from the buckets set into the corners of the platform. If the previous match was won by a man on the same side, that winner offers the wrestler *chikara mizu*, water of strength, which he uses to rinse out his mouth in purification. If the previous wrestler lost, then the next wrestler in line to fight hands up the ladle. Both combatants then wipe their mouths and upper bodies with a square of white *chikara-gami* (strength paper). Scooping a handful of salt from the baskets set at the corners of the ring, they turn and toss it into the center, then walk toward the middle of the ring. Some also put a grain or two on their tongues. The throwing of salt, *shio maki*, like the rituals with water and paper,

61. Asahikuni offers chikara mizu and chikara-gami to Wakanohana.

62. Wrestlers stamp on the ground before the match begins.

dates to the late seventeenth century, when Shinto purification rituals were adopted for use in public sumo tournaments. The ring is still considered a sacred battlefield—even today women are not allowed to step up onto the platform—and great importance is placed on purifying the arena prior to the tournaments. According to Shinto belief, salt has a cleansing power over evil spirits and defilement, in addition to being treasured for its healing properties. Following the completion of these first formalities, the two wrestlers squat on their heels facing one another, clap hands, and, in a chiri o kiru ritual like that of the yokozuna, each man rubs his hands together in front of him and brings them out at the sides with palms up, and then turned sharply down. The wrestlers then take a few steps forward, and, after stamping on the ground in the shiko, they squat behind the two parallel lines painted with white enamel in the center of the ring. The referee advances from the back of the ring and cries, "*Kamaete* (Take your places)!" and the wrestlers slowly lower their fists to the ground and crouch down, staring into each other's eyes. This is the shikiri, during which the wrestlers wait for the psychological right moment to charge. Invariably the contestants fail to come to that moment during the first shikiri, and they rise from their positions and return to their corners to take up another handful of salt. Before they return to their corners, there is often a staring match, *niramiai,* during which each man tries to intimidate the other. The amount of salt thrown varies from a mere pinch to a great handful, depending on the personality of the thrower. This series of motions will be repeated three to five times before the wrestlers actually begin to fight. Gone are the days, however, when an important match could be preceded by over an hour of *shikiri naoshi* (repeated shikiri) as the wrestlers waited for the right moment to begin. Since 1928, when live broadcasts of sumo began, strict time limits have been placed on the traditional prematch rituals. Today the shikiri, which is meant to allow the contestants to stabilize and concentrate both physically and spiritually, is limited to four minutes for makuuchi ranks, three minutes for juryo, and virtually nothing for those below, whose bouts must be over in two minutes. The wrestlers may begin the bout at any time within their time limit, provided that they synchronize their start. A start before the referee calls "time" (*jikan ippai*) is called *jikan mae*. When the time is up, the judge sitting under the giant red tassel signals the two announcers who are sitting at the corners with the salt and the water buckets. He also gives a nod to the referee when the latter glances over his shoulder to check the timing, while at the same time the two "seconds" get up and inform the wrestlers, offering them towels to refresh themselves.

63. Wrestlers crouching during the shikiri.

This time the referee's fan is held flat back against his body instead of out at the side, and now the match must begin. The two giants rush forward and slam together with awesome force in the tachiai, or initial charge. The referee darts about the ring, all the while crying out in a high-pitched voice, "*Nokotta, nokotta, nokotta* (You're still in)!" as long as the combatants are in motion, and an occasional "*Yoi! Hakkeyoi* (Get moving)!" when they stand locked in a grip, as each strains all his muscles in an effort to make the other fall first, every nerve alert to the slightest shift in the opponent's strategy. In almost astounding contrast to the lengthy warm-up period, a match itself is very often over in a matter of seconds. One wrestler may sidestep his opponent in the initial charge and slap him down immediately. Or the two may end up in a four-handed clinch, either on contact or after a series of slappings and pushings. Matches rarely last more than a minute or two at most, but on those occasions when the two wrestlers appear to have reached a stalemate, they are separated by the referee on the instructions of the chief judge, and retire to their corners for a short rest and a sip of water, from which the practice gets its name of *mizu iri*, or taking of water. The referee, who has been standing motionless with his eyes fixed on the places where the wrestlers last had their feet, then returns them to their former positions, assisted by shouted advice from the chief judge, who is receiving information over his earphone from a backstage judge watching the video screen. When everyone is satisfied that the two men are back to exactly where they were, the fight resumes. Sooner or later a foot touches outside the ring, an elbow hits the ground, or a three-hundred-pound wrestler lands squarely in the midst of the spectators sitting round the platform, and the match is over.

Ideally, there should be no show of emotion. The loser makes a short bow to his opponent and returns to the dressing room. The winner squats on his heels just in front of the straw bales on his side of the ring, and the referee with upraised fan declares him the victor. If patrons have donated prizes for the match, the referee squats down in front of the wrestler and extends a pile of envelopes on the flat of his fan. The wrestler makes three short chopping movements with his right hand, takes up the envelopes, gives a perfunctory bow, and climbs down. He then stands by the corner of the platform to offer in turn a ladle of water to the next wrestler on his side, after which he walks back down the aisle and through the crowd to the dressing room. During the changeover of a judges' shift, and at other times if necessary, yobidashi mount the platform to wet down and sweep the sandy surface. Immediately before each bout, the yobidashi who is doing the announcing gets up and sweeps a clear circle directly outside the ring of straw bales, so that in the event of a difficult decision, stray footprints will be more clearly visible.

Judges (*shobu shimpan*) sit on raised cushions on each of the four sides of the ring, their eyes being roughly level with the top surface of the platform. Dignified in their formal Japanese dress, *haori hakama*, they are all elders who in their day were well-known wrestlers themselves. The moment one of them sees a wrestler touch the surface, he holds up his right hand and shouts, in case the referee might not have observed the losing move. Judges have the authority to overturn any decision made by a referee. If one of the judges raises his hand in protest of a decision, the combatants climb down and retire to their corners as the judges climb into the ring to discuss the matter among themselves; this is known as the *mono ii*, or talking it over. Nowadays they usually invite the referee to give his reasoning, but it is not etiquette for him to present his case uninvited. After they return to their cushions, the head judge of the shift, who sits on the front side, announces the decision over the public address system. There are three possible decisions: *gumbai-dori* (according to the referee's fan, that is, his decision was correct); *sashichigai* (mistaken decision); and *torinaoshi*, a rematch, which includes all the preliminaries except the announcement of the contest. The judges usually have a better view than the referee, for no matter how quickly he moves about, the referee cannot always be in a clear position to see the crucial instant when a toe or an elbow touches the ground. A record is kept of each referee's sashichigai, and if he accumulates too many in the course of a year it may hold up his promotion. In extreme cases, a run of sashichigai can lead to suspension for the rest of a tournament. Even judges have been known to call a wrong decision, as photographs later proved. In such cases, however, the on-the-spot decision of the judges stands. After the particularly distressing mistake that broke Taiho's winning streak in March 1969, a new system was instituted whereby the head judge wears a tiny earphone connected to a room just outside the main hall, where two other judges study a closed-circuit videotape of the action. In matches below juryo this is not done, and the judges have to reach their decision unaided. There are four shifts of five judges, and the time of their duty rotates day by day. The first shift of the day appears only once, but the others do two shifts, reappearing in the same order in the juryo and makuuchi sections of the program. They also rotate their ringside positions each day, so that every judge has experience in seeing from all angles. For the upper-level bouts, one judge of the shift drops out and is replaced by one of the three chief judges, *shimpan bucho,* who always sits in the front position. Otherwise their positions are known as east, west, and, the two at the rear, "under the red tassel" (*aka-busa shita*) and "under the white tassel" (*shiro-busa shita*). The judge under the red tassel is always the timekeeper, and the referee awaiting his turn sits between the two at the rear. In former times the number of judges varied according to the rank of the bouts, but now there are five throughout an official tournament.

When the final match is over, a wrestler below juryo rank comes out to peform the *yumitori shiki,* or bow-taking ceremony, a bow-twirling exhibition that marks the end of the tournament day. It is customary for a makushita wrestler to be chosen, though demotion does not mean that he will lose the job. Although of a lower rank, he wears an embroidered apron and has his hair in the gingko-leaf style of the sekitori rank for this ceremony, which goes back over a thousand years. The winning wrestler at the annual Heian-court sumo tournament was presented with a bow after the final match, and the referee for his team performed a dance with it. The earliest documentation of the present bow-taking ceremony

64. Wakashimazu sends Asashio to the sand with a hataki komi on the fourteenth day of the January 1985 tournament.

65. Daigo performing the bow-taking ceremony after the last match of the day.

was in 1791, when the yokozuna Tanikaze was awarded a bow after winning the tournament held in Edo Castle in the presence of the eleventh Tokugawa shogun, Ienari, and flourished the bow in the four directions. In the public sumo tournaments in Edo, the awards—a bow for the winning ozeki, a bowstring for the sekiwake, and an arrow for the komusubi—were handed out on the final day of the performance, but until 1909 the highest-ranking wrestlers did not appear for the last day of matches. From 1796, on the tenth (at that time the final) day, a nidamme wrestler accepted the bow in place of the absent ozeki and flourished it in the ring. The ritual, known as the *yumi furi* (bow-waving), gradually became more complex, and makushita wrestlers specializing in the performance appeared. By the middle of the nineteenth century the ceremony was perfected in its present form. It was eliminated from the tournaments in 1946, only to be revived five years later. Since 1952 the ritual, which was previously performed only on the final day of a tournament, has been done every day at the end of the matches. It is the convention for the performer to enter the ring from the side of the winner of the last match.

The excitement of a tournament increases as the last day approaches and the battle for the championship intensifies. The last days pit the yokozuna and the ozeki together, unless a lower-ranking wrestler is in a position to win the championship. Until 1947, if two wrestlers were tied on the last day, the one with the higher rank was awarded the championship. Today there is a play-off match in the case of a tie. The wrestlers rest in the dressing room during the bow-taking ceremony and then return for the play-off. On the final day, those who will compete in the last three matches perform a small shikiri ceremony together before their bouts: the three from the east, followed by the three from the west, enter the ring and in unison do the foot-stamping and leg-raising. This is known as the *soroi-bumi*.

At the conclusion of the last match, a seemingly endless number of trophies and awards is handed out. All of the prizes go to individual wrestlers. Each division has its yusho, or championship, but the ranks from juryo down have their prize-giving ceremony earlier in the day, before the ring-entering ceremony of the makuuchi. The winner of the makuuchi yusho receives the Emperor's Cup, and a large banner is given to him by the sumo association. He also receives plaques and trophies from various public bodies and business organizations, and prizes in cash and in kind—a year's supply of gasoline, a bale of rice, a jar of dried mushrooms, giant bottles of whiskey—and the larger-than-life championship portrait presented by the Mainichi Press to be added to those exhibited around the ceiling of the Kokugikan, though this is not ready for presentation on the day. There are three special awards for makuuchi wrestlers under the rank of ozeki, and these are chosen by a group of elders and newspaper reporters. The Outstanding Performance Award goes to the man who upset the most yokozuna and ozeki, provided that his final score had more wins than losses; the Technique Award to the most skillful, and the Fighting Spirit Award for an especially laudable performance record. These awards may be withheld if no one has deserved them, or they may be shared by two men. It is also possible for one man to receive more than one award at a time. Each of these awards is worth half a million yen, compared with the two-million-yen of the championship prize.

Techniques Viewing sumo is more enjoyable when the spectator understands some of its subtleties, and knowing some of the basic holds and throws—or being able to recognize their names when the technique that determined a particular match is announced over the loudspeakers—is fundamental. The most common techniques have long been called the shijuhatte, or forty-eight hands. In 1960, however, the sumo association compiled an official list of seventy winning techniques. While it is claimed that there are over two hundred "hands" (*te*) in all, in practice only about forty are used with any frequency, and most wins are accounted for by a mere dozen or so. The numerous variations depend on whether the loser touches down inside or outside the ring, or the exact manner in which the winner slaps, pushes, pulls, or throws his opponent. There are three basic principles: *tsuki*, meaning slapping or thrusting; *oshi*, pushing; and *yori*, grappling or clinching. The following are some of the most commonly used techniques.

In the *tsuppari*, or slapping technique, both hands are open and used alternately and rapidly in an upward motion, hitting the opponent's chest, throat, or face, while the attacker simultaneously moves forward in an attempt to force the other man out of the ring. Success in this way is called *tsuki dashi* (thrust out). *Tsuki taoshi* (thrust down) means that the opponent has been forced down inside the ring by using the slapping method. A wrestler may defend himself against a tsuki technique by pushing the attacker's hands up before they make contact or by twisting out of the way. *Tsuki otoshi* is a move that forces an opponent who has an arm inside one's own off balance by twisting the body and thrusting downward on his side or arm. *Hataki komi* is sidestepping a charge and then slapping the attacker down while he is momentarily off balance. *Hikkake* is stepping to the side of the arm the attacker used first in the thrust, grabbing that outstretched arm, and pulling it forward in the same direction until the staggering opponent falls or steps out of the ring. *Okuri dashi* means to dodge a thrusting attack used at the very beginning of a match, get behind the attacker, and push him out of the ring. *Okuri taoshi* is the same as okuri dashi but is used to pull the opponent down in the ring. *Te yotsu* is when both wrestlers come to a sudden deadlock during a bout of thrusting and counterthrusting by holding each other's hands. Usually the slapping technique is used at the very beginning of a match, immediately following the charge, although sometimes it will begin after the wrestlers separate momentarily following the failure of a different maneuver. Often an attacker can render his opponent helpless with a tsuki technique and force him out of the ring within seconds of the initial charge.

Pushing is done with the palm open and the thumb and forefinger spread wide when against the chin, throat, or armpit of an opponent. It is devastating when used by a tall wrestler against the chin of a shorter opponent, as it effectively keeps the latter from getting any kind of a grip on the pusher's belt. A short wrestler

COMMON SUMO
WINNING TECHNIQUES

The following are some of the most common
sumo throws. The wrestler in black is the
victor in each of the illustrations.

YORI KIRI

UWATE NAGE

SHITATE NAGE

OSHI DASHI

TSUKI DASHI

SOTO-GAKE

UCHI-GAKE

NODOWA

HIKKAKE

UTCHARI

SUKUI NAGE

KOTE NAGE

TSURI DASHI

OKURI DASHI

TSUKI OTOSHI

HATAKI KOMI

can, however, push a taller opponent with one hand in the pit of the other's arm. To get away from such moves, a man must first push upward on the opponent's elbow and then inward on the elbow from outside while twisting away, or, if he can, push the opponent away at the throat, a move known as *nodowa* (throat push). When a man is pushed out of the ring, the win is an *oshi dashi* (pushed out). When a wrestler is pushed down, whether in or out of the ring, it is called an *oshi taoshi* (pushed down). In addition, there are a number of other techniques employing pushing or used in defense against it; fast and skillful footwork is needed to execute them to advantage.

Grappling or clinching, with each wrestler clinging to the other's belt with both hands, is sometimes arrived at immediately upon charging, but more often it follows a series of thrustings and pushings. In grappling, the heavier wrestler has the advantage, for he can use his greater weight to gradually edge his opponent out of the ring. The goal in grappling techniques is to get one's stronger arm on the inside of the opponent's; usually one arm is on the inside and the other is on the outside. If the right arm is on the inside during a clinch, it is called *migi yotsu,* and if the left is inside, *hidari yotsu.* If both arms are under those of the opponent, the grip is known as *morozashi.* And when a wrestler reaches over his opponent's arm or shoulder to get an outside hold on the belt, the grip is called *uwate.*

The most common of all the winning techniques is *yori kiri* (forcing out), in which one wrestler forces the other outside the ring by getting a firm grip on his opponent's belt and pushing. *Yori taoshi* (forcing out and down) is when the losing wrestler is thrown down as he is pushed out of the ring. When a wrestler works both his arms under those of his opponent and manages to lift him up, bending his body backward, and carry him out of the ring, the win is called *tsuri dashi* (lifting out). *Tsuri otoshi* (lifting and forcing down) means the opponent is pushed down onto his knees by a wrestler who has a grip on his belt. *Kake* techniques use the leg to unbalance an opponent while grappling. *Uchi-gake* (inner-leg tripping) is done by wrapping one's leg from the inside around that of one's opponent, and *soto-gake* (outer-leg tripping) is done from the outside. *Nage* techniques employ the hips to maneuver and throw an opponent, with or without a grip on his belt. *Kote nage* (forearm throw) is carried out by grasping the opponent's arm that is on the inside in a grip and shifting one's body with a twist of the hip to throw the opponent by bending forward and pulling him down. *Uwate nage* (outer-arm throw) is similar to kote nage, but the wrestler using the technique has an outer grip on the belt. *Shitate nage* (inner-arm throw) uses an inner grip on the belt to throw the opponent, *sukui nage* (scooping throw) unbalances with an arm scooped across the opponent's back, and *kubi nage* (neck throw) uses an arm around the neck. *Hineri* techniques are employed to twist the opponent off balance by first pulling him in either by the outer hand (*uwate hineri*) or inner hand (*shitate hineri*) and then twisting him to one side and throwing him down.

Sometimes when a wrestler finds himself forced to the edge of the ring in a grip and seems certain to lose, a stunning defensive technique is employed. This is *utchari* (throwing down at the edge of the ring) and is executed by the apparent loser's suddenly bending backward as far as possible, lifting his opponent off the ground, and throwing him out of the ring by turning his own body to one side. This technique, however, carries great risk of injury, and although very popular with the crowd it is very much a last-ditch effort.

The only exceptions to the rule that the wrestler who touches the ground inside or outside the ring first loses are that when a man lifts his opponent into the air and out of the ring, he can carry him out, stepping beyond the edge of the ring himself (*okuri ashi*), and that if there is a possibility of injury when the two men fall in the ring at the same time, the one on top may break the fall by putting his hand to the ground to support some of his weight (*kabaite*).

Schedule A famous Edo-period satirical poem once described wrestlers as "fellows who earn a year's living in twenty days of work." At the time, to be sure, there were only two tournaments a year. Indeed, until 1909, wrestlers of the makuuchi rank took part in only nine of the ten days of a tournament. On the surface the life of the wrestler was an enviable one. In practice, however, the periods between tournaments were spent almost without break on the road giving provincial performances or in intensive practice in the stable, and it was only the rare professional wrestler who was able to spend more than a handful of days a year at home with his wife and children—if he had time to have any. Today is little different, for with the number of annual tournaments increased threefold and the hurried tempo of postwar Japan, life for the wrestler has, if anything, become even more regimented and harried.

In former days *jungyo*, or provincial touring, was done by small groups of wrestlers, usually by stables. In 1957, however, the sumo association decreed that touring should be done in principle by the entire body of upper-ranking wrestlers. Generally the provincial matches are more relaxing for the sekitori-level wrestlers than are the six major tournaments, for these tours have no bearing whatsoever on the wrestlers' rankings or pay. For those apprentices who go on tour, however, the provincial performances are even more hectic than life in the stable. Each day a "tournament" is held in a different location, and when a local gymnasium is not available, the apprentices must set up temporary dressing rooms for the sekitori, in addition to preparing cooking areas and hauling the equipment from the trucks that travel from town to town carrying tournament necessities. When the matches are over, everything has to be taken down and the trucks repacked. In transportation there is no letup in stable discipline, and apprentice wrestlers must walk to the train station, carrying both their own luggage and that of their seniors, while the sekitori leave by taxi or bus. The sumo association usually charters its own train, with first-class cars reserved for the highest-ranking wrestlers and the elders traveling with them. Even at the inns or private homes at which the wrestlers are put up while on tour, the younger wrestlers must help out in serving meals and taking care of their assigned sekitori. Life is no picnic for the apprentice in the provinces, but the hard work often gives him an edge over the other apprentices who have stayed behind in the stable, having not been assigned as tsukebito to one of the sekitori men.

The year for the wrestler begins with a holiday, albeit a very brief one, for the New Year. Apart from the stable-only party, there may be some event that includes supporters, for example, a rice-cake-pounding party; but practice soon resumes, for the January tournament begins on the second Sunday of the month. After every tournament the wrestlers all get a week's rest. If there are retirement ceremonies, they take place on the weekend following the Tokyo tournaments. On the Friday, or on the weekend if there is no retirement scheduled, NHK sponsors a charity performance in January, and TV Asahi does the same after the September tournament. These charity shows began in 1967.

The name for these informal performances is *hana-zumo*, a term which originated in the mid-Edo period, when wrestlers performed for donations (*hana*) rather than charging entrance fees, since the Tokugawa government had prohibited the latter. Hana was a term used to describe congratulatory gifts, and indicated rewards received by artists in general. Later the character meaning flower (*hana*) was adopted to replace the original character, which had been borrowed from the Chinese during the Heian period.

Hana-zumo tournaments include regular matches between high-ranking wrestlers—which, like provincial tour matches, do not count on a man's record—but most of the show is meant to be informal and entertaining for audience and wrestlers alike. There are *gonin nuki* matches, in which a top wrestler must defeat five opponents in rapid succession; exhibitions of drumming techniques by a yobidashi; and demonstrations of dressing a wrestler's hair and tying the yokozuna knot. Half-a-dozen junior wrestlers borrow ceremonial aprons from their seniors and, forming a circle, take turns to sing special sumo songs called *jinku*. One of the highlights of hana-zumo is always the *shokkiri*, a comedy match performed by two makushita wrestlers who kick and slap each other about the ring, using forbidden holds and humorous gestures. All these performers receive a fee for their services, and the names of the sponsors are printed in the program. Sometimes there are matches between popular wrestlers and small boys, occasionally including foreign ones.

When a sekitori who has acquired elder stock retires, a hana-zumo performance, also known as intai-zumo, is held. The main event is a haircutting ceremony (*dampatsu shiki*). If it is a yokozuna who is retiring, he performs his final ring-entering ceremony flanked by the other incumbent yokozuna, or an ozeki if there is only one other yokozuna. Three yokozuna in their white ropes together is an impressive and emotional sight. For the haircutting itself, the retiree sits in formal Japanese dress on a chair in the ring. Then a seemingly interminable number of the wrestler's patrons step up into the ring to take a snip at the projecting base of the hair style, under the direction of the stable's highest-ranking referee or the chief referee, who holds a plain wooden Shinto-style offering tray with gold-plated scissors throughout the ceremony. Each snipper has paid a handsome donation for the privilege. At the end of the long line come the man's fellow wrestlers and sumo association officials before the stablemaster finally ascends to cut the topknot completely free and place it on the wooden tray. The proceeds of intai-zumo, which otherwise is the same as the charity shows, go to the retiring wrestler.

The general pattern of the sumo year remains the same, although outside of the official tournaments the details vary: one week's rest after a tournament, followed by some kind of tour or other exhibition by the sekitori divisions, while the junior wrestlers not wanted on tour continue training in their stables, until two weeks before the next tournament, when all go into serious training, either in Tokyo or in temporary quarters in the city where the next tournament will be held. Since 1977, an unofficial two-day tournament has been held in February. In 1983, it was sponsored by Fuji Television, Bunka Hoso, and a sakè company. Unlike official tournaments, which are called hombasho in Japanese, it is known by the English word, pronounced *toonamento* in Japanese. After it, short tours are usual.

The Osaka tournament begins on the second Sunday of March, and it is followed by a tour of the Kinki and Chubu regions, including a ceremonial appearance at the Grand Shrine of Ise. The group gradually returns to Tokyo in time for the annual performance at the Yasukuni Shrine in Tokyo in honor of the war dead. That is in the third week in April. The May tournament in Tokyo begins on the second Sunday of the month, to be followed by retirement ceremonies but not a charity performance. June sees minor tours and personal appearances, but it is generally a rather slack period that affords a suitable time for overseas tours—though these may happen at other times too. They are most often to Hawaii and the continental United States, though tours and promotional appearances have been made in a number of other countries, including China in 1973 and, more recently, Mexico in 1981. The Nagoya tournament in July is the only one to start on the first Sunday of the month. Following it there is a very important tour of Hokkaido and the Tohoku region. After Hokkaido, it is normal for the party to be divided into two groups so as to cover as much ground as possible. They return to Tokyo in late August in time for the September tournament preparations. October sees another long tour, with the party gradually moving southwestward, taking a detour through Shikoku, and then crossing over into Kyushu two weeks before the start of the last tournament of the year, in Fukuoka. Following that tournament and the regular week's rest, the lower divisions return as usual by slow train to Tokyo, while the sekitori ranks go on a final tour round Kyushu, returning to Tokyo in mid-December via a few places on the Inland Sea. This marks the end of the sumo year.

Stables

THE THIRTY-SEVEN SUMO STABLES vary in size and prestige. Generally a "great" stable tends to remain great, for one that produces high-ranking wrestlers is likely to attract not only valuable patrons but also new apprentices who have championship potential. The following are short histories of fourteen of the most powerful stables, all of which have consistently trained wrestlers of juryo and makuuchi rank in recent decades. Some of these stables were founded about two hundred years ago.

Dewanoumi   The Dewanoumi stable was begun by a wrestler named Dewanoumi Ren'emon, who was active in Edo during the last two decades of the eighteenth century. Both he and his successor were born in the Dewanokuni region of Yamagata Prefecture. The third-generation Dewanoumi was a wrestler by the name of Hitachiyama who assumed the stable name in 1861. His own successor—also a Hitachiyama—produced a third Hitachiyama, who became the great Meiji-era yokozuna and the first of that rank to travel to the United States and Europe. He later inherited the stable as the fifth Dewanoumi and trained a total of thirty-seven makuuchi wrestlers, establishing the stable as the largest and most powerful in the sumo world. The sixth and seventh generations—the ozeki Ryogoku and the yokozuna Tsunenohana—continued to produce outstanding wrestlers. On the death of Tsunenohana, the elder Musashigawa, who was acting as an adviser to the stable, took over as master. When he was elected head of the sumo association in 1968, he had again become Musashigawa, and had passed the stable on to the former yokozuna Sadanoyama, who is the ninth-generation Dewanoumi. Current sekitori wrestlers of this stable are Dewanohana, Sadanoumi, Onishiki, and Washuyama. The former yokozuna Mienoumi Tsuyoshi now holds the Musashigawa name, and has his own stable.

Futagoyama The earliest mention, dated 1791, of the name Futagoyama appeared in the records of the shogunal sumo performance held in Edo Castle that year. In 1922 a wrestler from the Tomozuna stable by the name of Toshuyama, who was one of Hitachiyama's most persistent rivals, adopted the name as the eighth-generation elder. He remained in the sumo association until he died at the age of seventy-one in 1960, at which time his elder name was passed on to the yokozuna Wakanohana, a wrestler of the Hanakago stable. Wakanohana did not actually retire until over a year later and during that time rented out his elder stock to the wrestler Onoura. Wakanohana was thus formally considered the tenth-generation Futagoyama when he began a stable of that name in 1962. Among his star wrestlers have been his younger brother, the ozeki Takanohana; the yokozuna Wakanohana II (formerly known by the name Wakamisugi); the yokozuna Takanosato; the ozeki (as of January 1985) Wakashimazu; and an impressive string of other makuuchi men.

Hanakago The first Hanakago was active in Edo sumo in the mid-1720s. The third through sixth generations were all wrestlers born in the Niigata region, while the eighth-generation Hanakago, who succeeded to the name in 1909, was the well-known Meiji-era ozeki Araiwa. He was followed by a Taisho wrestler by the name of Misugiiso. The tenth generation, Terunishiki, was replaced by a wrestler of the Nishonoseki stable, Onoumi, after Misugiiso's widow exerted her influence to have him ousted in 1953. As related before, Onoumi took with him some of his stablemates, including the Wakanohana who is now master of Futagoyama stable. He broke with tradition by moving west to Asagaya to build a new stable. On his retirement in March 1981 he was succeeded by his son-in-law, the yokozuna Wajima, and died of cancer the following September, just before Wajima's formal retirement ceremony.

As Wajima's stablemaster, he would have been expected to make the final cut that removed the topknot of hair; instead, his portrait was carried into the ring by his eldest son while the cutting was performed by his most distinguished ex-deshi, Futagoyama. Other famous past wrestlers of the stable include the ozeki Kaiketsu, and Arase, Ryuko, and Wakanoumi.

Isegahama   The name Isegahama was first adopted by a late-Edo-period wrestler, Arakuma, who retired in 1859 to establish his own stable. He was followed in the early Meiji era by Ryogoku Kajino-suke. In the late 1910s Tsurugahama took over, and he was suc-ceeded by the Taisho-era sekiwake Kiyosegawa. Among the many high-ranking wrestlers of his stable was the yokozuna Terukuni, who became the fifth-generation Isegahama and whose own apprentices included Kurosegawa. Terukuni died in 1977 and was replaced by Kiyokuni. Current wrestlers are Wakasegawa and Takarakuni (previously Saisu).

Isenoumi   The first Isenoumi was a wrestler who bore this name during the 1740s. One of the central figures in the establishment of the Edo sumo association in the latter half of the eighteenth century, he set a pattern of leadership in the sumo world for successive generations of Isenoumi masters. Tanikaze Kajinosuke was an early member of the stable. With the third generation, a tradition was established whereby the chosen successor to the stable would wrestle under the name of Kashiwado. The previous Isenoumi, like those before him, was a Kashiwado. His own chosen successor, who became yokozuna in 1961, retired in 1969 to revive the Ka-gamiyama stable, so that the present Isenoumi, who succeeded on the death of his predecessor in 1983, did not in fact hold the name Kashiwado. The stable is at present a very small one.

Kasugano   The first Kasugano was born in the Akita region and was active in Edo during the 1750s. The name was not revived until 1844, sixty-two years after his death, and it was then that the stable was founded. The seventh-generation master was a Kimura referee, who was succeeded by one of the wrestlers, the yokozuna Tochigiyama, in 1926. He in turn trained the yokozuna To-chinishiki and Tochinoumi and the ozeki Tochihikari. Tochinishiki took over the stable in 1960. Current wrestlers include another Tochihikari (Kaneshiro), Tochiakagi, former college champion Masudayama, and Hachiya, to name but a few.

Kataonami The first Kataonami was an early-eighteenth-century wrestler. The name was dropped from the rolls of the sumo association with his death and did not reappear until 1846. The ninth-generation mastership went to Kamikaze Shoichi, who later became a popular commentator for NHK. Tamanoumi of the Nishonoseki stable took over as the twelfth-generation master in 1961. One of his apprentices was the late yokozuna Tamanoumi. Tamanofuji, and Tamakiyama, now retired, were members of this stable. The only current sekitori is Tamaryu.

Kokonoe The Kokonoe name first appeared over two hundred and twenty years ago. In the late Edo period a wrestler of the Urakaze stable took on the name, while again in 1887 the name was revived by the wrestler Uraminato as the sixth-generation Kokonoe. He was followed in 1904 by Maedagawa, one of his own apprentices. The two following generations, Ichinohama and Toyokuni, were both wrestlers of the Izutsu stable; Toyokuni was later replaced by a coach of the Dewanoumi stable. After he died in 1952, the wrestler Oedo rented the position for almost seven years until the yokozuna Chiyonoyama retired to become the twelfth-generation Kokonoe. He severed his ties with the Dewanoumi stable in early 1967 to form a new stable, taking with him a number of high-ranking wrestlers. Chiyonoyama trained the yokozuna Kitanofuji and, in his early days, the present yokozuna Chiyonofuji. Chiyonoyama died in 1977. Kitanofuji, at that time Izutsu oyakata and master of the newly founded Izutsu stable, took over the more prestigious name and amalgamated the two stables. The master of Kimogahama stable acquired the Izutsu stock and name, but his stable changed in name only. Among recent and current wrestlers of the Kokonoe stable are Kitaseumi, Shiratayama, Hoshi, Wakanofuji, and yokozuna Chiyonofuji.

Mihogaseki One of the most famous elder names in Osaka sumo is Mihogaseki. The name first appeared in 1743 as Miogaseki; by the end of the Edo period, however, the present form had become the accepted reading of the characters used to write it. The sixth and seventh generations led the Osaka sumo association, but the eighth-generation Mihogaseki moved the stable to Tokyo in 1927. His apprentice and successor, the ozeki Masuiyama, took the name in 1950 and trained a large number of high-ranking wrestlers, restoring a semblance of its former power to the stable. His apprentices have included his own son, also an ozeki, Masuiyama; yokozuna Kitanoumi, ozeki Hokutenyu, and sekitori Toryu and

Banryuyama. In 1984, the son succeeded his father as the tenth-generation Mihogaseki.

Nishonoseki This stable was founded in 1806 by the wrestler Nishikigi. He was retained by the Nambu lords, who traditionally bestowed the name Nishonoseki—a famous local barrier station—on their wrestlers. The sixth-generation Nishonoseki was the yokozuna Tamanishiki, who trained many sekitori. Four of them subsequently left the stable to become the masters of the Hanakago, Sadogatake, Kataonami, and Futagoyama stables. The seventh-generation master was Tamanoumi, who later became a well-known commentator for NHK. The ozeki Saganohana succeeded to the position of stablemaster in 1951. He died in 1975 and after a period of uncertainty was succeeded by the maegashira Kongo, who had secured the post by his marriage to Saganohana's daughter. The most famous wrestler of this stable was the yokozuna Taiho, who is now master of his own Taiho stable; the former ozeki Daikirin has also founded his own stable, the Oshiogawa. Current wrestlers are Kirinji, Daitetsu, and Ho-o.

Sadogatake The Sadogatake stable was begun by an early Edo elder who was a retainer of the Matsu lords of the Unshu area. Because so many of its wrestlers came from the area, it was also known as the Unshu stable. In the first half of the nineteenth century it produced the yokozuna Inazuma, but soon after it began to decline. The tenth-generation Sadogatake, however, trained the yokozuna Minanogawa, and his successor, the Nishonoseki stable wrestler Kotonishiki, who took over in 1955, produced the ozeki Kotogahama. The present master is the former yokozuna Kotozakura; recent and current wrestlers include Hasegawa, Kotonofuji, and the ozeki Kotokaze.

Takasago Takasago Uragoro, who led the reform movement in the organization of the sumo association shortly after the Meiji Restoration, was the nineteenth-century wrestler who began the Takasago stable. While he was master the stable produced a number of famous wrestlers, making it the most powerful in Tokyo. It lost that standing during the anti-Takasago movement of 1896, although the stable continued to prosper generation after generation. The fourth Takasago was the former Maedayama, who inherited the stable in 1942 while still an active wrestler. He became yokozuna five years later and did not retire to take over the stable until 1949. At his death in 1971 the position of stablemaster passed to the former yokozuna Asashio, then acting as coach under the name Furiwake. The stable is noted for introducing the Hawaiian wrestler Takamiyama and, more recently, the Hawaiian-Samoan Konishiki. Also well-known are the veteran Fujizakura and the former college champion Nagaoka, who received the name Asashio from his master.

Tatsunami The Tatsunami stable was started in 1916 by the fourth-generation holder of that name. He trained the yokozuna Futabayama and Haguroyama, as well as a total of nearly thirty makuuchi wrestlers. He was succeeded by Haguroyama in 1954, who in turn was followed by a man of the same name in 1969. Former wrestlers include the ozeki Asahikuni, now master of his own Oshima stable; the sekiwake Kurohimeyama; and komusubi Haguroiwa, who, under his own name, Toda, was incorrectly assigned the win that broke Taiho's winning streak.

Tokitsukaze The name Tokitsukaze was a prominent one in Osaka sumo more than two centuries ago. The sixth-generation Tokitsukaze led the Osaka sumo organization from the end of the Edo period to the middle of the Meiji era. The twelfth-generation master, who took the name in 1921, moved the stable to Tokyo. After retiring in 1946, the yokozuna Futabayama adopted the name Tokitsukaze and became master. Under his guidance the stable produced a great many successful wrestlers, including the yokozuna Kagamisato and the ozeki Ouchiyama, Kitabayama, and Yutakayama. He was later elected director of the sumo association and succeeded in pushing through a number of reforms in the organization. After his death in 1968, Yutakayama succeeded him, becoming the fourteenth Tokitsukaze. Well-known recent and current wrestlers include a second Yutakayama, Futatsuryu, Kurama, Oyutaka, Amanoyama (real name Ogata), and the veteran Oshio.

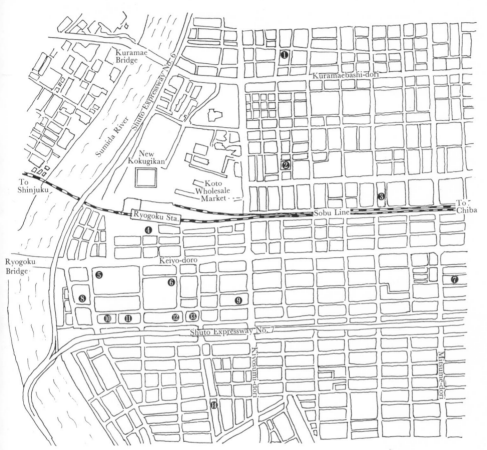

Numbers in parentheses refer to stables appearing on the map of the Ryogoku area.

Ajigawa
1–7–4 Mori
Koto-ku, Tokyo 135
634–5515

Asahiyama
4–14–21 Kita Kasai
Edogawa-ku, Tokyo 134
687–8321

Dewanoumi (11)
2–3–15 Ryogoku
Sumida-ku, Tokyo 130
631–0090

Fujishima
3–10–6 Honcho
Nakano-ku, Tokyo 164
372–7756

Futagoyama
3–25–10 Narita Higashi
Suginami-ku, Tokyo 166
317–0018

Hanakago
3–10–22 Asagaya Minami
Suginami-ku, Tokyo 166
398–9625

Hanaregoma
3–12–7 Asagaya Minami
Suginami-ku, Tokyo 166
392–5010

Isegahama
5–7–14 Hakusan
Bunkyo-ku, Tokyo 112
945–0150

Isenoumi
3–8–80 Harue-cho
Edogawa-ku, Tokyo 132
676–3386

Izutsu (10)
2–2–7 Ryogoku
Sumida-ku, Tokyo 130
633–8920

Kagamiyama
8–16–1 Kita Koiwa
Edogawa-ku, Tokyo 133
673–5358

Kasugano (8)
1–7–11 Ryogoku
Sumida-ku, Tokyo 130
631–1871

Kasugayama
1–10–14 Saga
Koto-ku, Tokyo 135
630–4322

Kataonami (1)
1–33–9 Ishiwara
Sumida-ku, Tokyo 130
625–6087

Kise
2–35–21 Hongo
Bunkyo-ku, Tokyo 113
815–2771

Kokonoe (2)
1–16–1 Kamezawa
Sumida-ku, Tokyo 130
621–1800

Kumagatani
1–6–28 Minami Koiwa
Edogawa-ku, Tokyo 133
658–2465

Magaki (3)
3–8–1 Kamezawa
Sumida-ku, Tokyo 130
623–8865

Michinoku
3–13–14 Hirai
Edogawa-ku, Tokyo 132
637–3434

Mihogaseki (14)
3–2–12 Chitose
Sumida-ku, Tokyo 130
631–3067

Minato
2–20–10 Shibanakata
Kawaguchi-shi, Saitama-ken 333
(0482) 65–1500

Miyagino (7)
4–16–3 Midori
Sumida-ku, Tokyo 130
632–8335

Musashigawa
3–2–9 Hirano
Koto-ku, Tokyo 135
643–9383

Nishonoseki (9)
4–17–1 Ryogoku
Sumida-ku, Tokyo 130
631–7502

Onaruto
2–22–14 Kitakata
Ichikawa-shi, Chiba-ken 272
(0473) 35–3169

Oshima (12)
3–5–3 Ryogoku
Sumida-ku, Tokyo 130
632–0240

Oshiogawa
2-17-7 Kiba
Koto-ku, Tokyo 135
643-9797

Oyama
5-35-13 Higashi Koiwa
Edogawa-ku, Tokyo 133
673-5603

Sadogatake
4-18-13 Taihei
Sumida-ku, Tokyo 130
626-2875

Taiho
2-8-3 Kiyosumi
Koto-ku, Tokyo 135
641-0027

Takadagawa
2-1-15 Ichinoe
Edogawa-ku, Tokyo 132
656-0015

Takasago
1-22-5 Yanagibashi
Taito-ku, Tokyo 111
861-4600

Tatsunami (4)
3-26-2 Ryogoku
Sumida-ku, Tokyo 130
632-1138

Tatsutagawa (13)
4-7-11 Ryogoku
Sumida-ku, Tokyo 130
631-9336

Tokitsukaze (6)
3-15-3 Ryogoku
Sumida-ku, Tokyo 130
635-0015

Tomozuna
1-20-7 Mori
Koto-ku, Tokyo 135
631-0135

Wakamatsu (5)
2-10-8 Ryogoku
Sumida-ku, Tokyo 130
635-1044

Information on sumo is available (in Japanese) through
the Japan Sumo Association at:

Nihon Sumo Kyokai
(Japan Sumo Association)
1-3-28 Yokoami
Sumida-ku, Tokyo 130
623-5111

Chart of Yokozuna

THE RANK OF YOKOZUNA remained a merely honorary appellation long after Tanikaze and Onogawa were presented with the first yokozuna licenses in 1789. In fact, the characters for yokozuna were not even used on a program until 1890, and then it was another thirteen years before the term came to be accepted as generally defining the highest-ranking wrestler on each team. Official recognition came even later, however, for it was only in 1909, when the Kokugikan in Ryogoku was first opened, that the sumo association finally issued a statute officially stating that the rank of yokozuna was the highest position in sumo.

The term yokozuna had been around for a long while by that time, however, and in 1895 the former yokozuna Jimmaku Kyugoro decided to compile a list of all the historical yokozuna through Nishinoumi Kajiro I, who was the sixteenth. But his was no easy task, for in addition to having to dig through confusing, incomplete, and often contradictory documentary evidence, Jimmaku also had to delve into the problem of *hinoshita kaizan,* a term that was used almost interchangeably with the appellation "yokozuna" during the late Edo period and the early Meiji era and that was generally taken to indicate the equivalent in status to yokozuna.

Hinoshita kaizan was a phrase that originated in the Muromachi period to honor the founders of Buddhist temples: *hinoshita* (or *hishita*) meant first under the sun, while the *kaizan* referred to the founder of a religious order. Later the phrase was extended to include artisans and practitioners of the martial arts, and by the middle of the Edo period it had become an honorific title for champion sumo wrestlers. At first, any champion who remained undefeated for a long period of time was praised as hishita kaizan, but by the end of the Edo period the term was used solely to describe a wrestler of yokozuna status.

All of this presented a good many problems for Jimmaku when he tried to compile his list. In the final draft Jimmaku included three wrestlers who had been known as hishita kaizan: Akashi Shiganosuke, Ayagawa Goroji, and Maruyama Gontazaemon. Akashi was a well-known but apparently fictitious figure from narratives published in the latter half of the Edo period. Ayagawa also seemed to fall into the same category, and there is no evidence that, even if he was an actual wrestler, he ever received a yokozuna license.

Jimmaku's compilation came under attack almost immediately. Some of his contemporaries demanded that the Genroku-era wrestlers Ryogoku Kajinosuke or Genjiyama Yokogoro be inserted in place of Ayagawa, and the Yoshida family of referees officially recognized Genjiyama until the mid-1920s. And many insisted that Tanikaze be listed as the first historical yokozuna, which he certainly was.

Jimmaku's list was publicly announced in 1900, but the controversy surrounding it continued for years, and it was not until 1926 that it was finally accepted as correct and came to be the pattern by which all later yokozuna were numbered.

Lists of yokozuna available today in Japanese and English still show some discrepancies. The chart below was compiled by comparing several of these sources and selecting the most frequently agreed upon data. Many wrestlers belonged to more than one stable and held several elder names, but only the last of each is given. Only victories in Tokyo tournaments are listed, and ties are not counted among total championships. Heights and weights indicate the peak reached during the wrestler's professional career for retired wrestlers, and the highest to date for still active wrestlers. These figures vary the most from source to source, but usually only by a few centimeters or kilograms—the units in which all are recorded.

No.	Name	Birth/Death	Native Prefecture	Ht./Wt.	Stable	Deb
1	Akashi Shiganosuke	17 c. ?/?	Tochigi?	?/?	—	?
2	Ayagawa Goroji	1700?/?	Tochigi?	?/?	—	?
3	Maruyama Gontazaemon	1713?/1749	Miyagi	?/?	—	?
4	Tanikaze Kajinosuke	1750/1795	Miyagi	189/169	Sekinoto	1769
5	Onogawa Kisaburo	1758/1806	Shiga	176/116	Onogawa††	1779
6	Onomatsu Midorinosuke	1791/1851	Ishikawa	173/135	Takekuma	1816
7	Inazuma Raigoro	1795/1877	Ibaraki	188/142	Sadogatake	1821
8	Shiranui Dakuemon	1801/1854	Kumamoto	176/135	Urakaze	1830
9	Hidenoyama Raigoro	1808/1862	Miyagi	164/135	Hidenoyama	1828
10	Unryu Hisakichi	1823/1891	Fukuoka	179/135	Oitekaze	1847
11	Shiranui Koemon	1825/1879	Kumamoto	176/124	Sakaigawa	1850
12	Jimmaku Kyugoro	1829/1903	Shimane	174/139	Hidenoyama	1851
13	Kimenzan Tanigoro	1826/1871	Gifu	186/149	Takekuma	1852
14	Sakaigawa Namiemon	1843/1889	Chiba	176/128	Sakaigawa	1857
15	Umegatani Totaro I	1845/1928	Fukuoka	176/124	Tamagaki	1871
16	Nishinoumi Kajiro I	1855/1908	Kagoshima	176/128	Takasago	1882
17	Konishiki Yasokichi	1867/1914	Chiba	168/143	Takasago	1883
18	Ozutsu Man'emon	1870/1918	Miyagi	197/131	Oguruma	1885
19	Hitachiyama Taniemon	1874/1922	Ibaraki	174/147	Dewanoumi	1891
20	Umegatani Totaro II	1878/1927	Toyama	168/158	Ikazuchi	1891
21	Wakashima Gonshiro††	1876/1943	Chiba	178/116	Tachiyama	1890
22	Tachiyama Mine'emon	1877/1941	Toyama	188/150	Tomozuna	1900
23	Okido Moriemon††	1877/1916	Hyogo	177/120	Minato	1897
24	Otori Tanigoro	1887/1956	Chiba	174/112	Miyagino	1903
25	Nishinoumi Kajiro II	1880/1931	Kagoshima	185/135	Izutsu	1900
26	Onishiki Uichiro	1891/1941	Osaka-fu	175/143	Dewanoumi	1910
27	Tochigiyama Moriya	1892/1959	Tochigi	172/103	Dewanoumi	1911
28	Onishiki Daigoro††	1883/1943	Aichi	176/113	Asahiyama	1903

† *Died while still an active wrestler.*
** *Retired from the sumo world.*
†† *Active in Osaka sumo.*

ʼOKOZUNA

Promoted to Ozeki	Promoted to Yokozuna	Makuuchi Record: Wins	Losses	Highest No. Successive Wins	Total Championships	Year Retired	Elder Name
—	—			?	?	?	—
—	—	?	?	?	?	?	—
c. 1730	·1749?	?	?	?	?	?	—
1781	1789	258	14	63	21	†	
—	1789	144	13	32	7	1798	††
1826	1828	140	31	19	5	1835	Ononomatsu
1828	1830	130	13	33	10	1839	**
1839	1842	48	15	16	1	1844	Minato††
1841	1845	112	21	30	6	1850	Hidenoyama
1858	1861	127	32	15	7	1865	Oitekaze
1862	1863	119	35	16	3	1869	Minato††
1866	1867	87	5	25	5	1867	††
1865	1869	143	24	21	7	1870	
1870	1876	118	23	26	5	1881	Sakaigawa
1879	1884	116	6	58	9	1885	Ikazuchi
1885	1890	127	37	14	2	1896	Izutsu
1890	1896	119	24	39	7	1900	Hatachiyama
1899	1901	98	29	20	2	1908	Matsuchiyama
1901	1903	150	15	32	8	1914	Dewanoumi
1900	1903	168	27	19	3	1915	Ikazuchi
1901	1905	87	33	28		1907	**
1909	1911	195	27	54	11	1918	**
1905	1912	143	20	28		1914	Minato††
1913	1915	108	49	14	2	1920	Miyagino††
1910	1916	136	38	14	1	1918	Izutsu
1916	1917	119	16	28	5	1923	**
1917	1918	166	23	29	9	1925	Kasugano
1910	1918	158	48			1923	**

No.	Name	Birth/Death	Native Prefecture	Ht./Wt.	Stable	Dea
29	Miyagiyama Fukumatsu	1895/1943	Iwate	173/113	Tokadagawa	191(
30	Nishinoumi Kajiro III	1890/1933	Kagoshima	185/124	Izutsu	191(
31	Tsunenohana Kan'ichi	1896/1960	Okayama	177/117	Dewanoumi	191(
32	Tamanishiki San'emon	1903/1938	Kochi	173/135	Nishonoseki	191!
33	Musashiyama Takeshi	1909/1969	Kanagawa	186/120	Dewanoumi	192(
34	Minanogawa Tozo	1903/1971	Ibaraki	193/154	Takasago	1924
35	Futabayama Sadaji	1912/1968	Oita	178/134	Tatsunami	192'
36	Haguroyama Masaji	1914/1969	Niigata	178/139	Tatsunami	1934
37	Akinoumi Setsu	1914/1979	Hiroshima	177/129	Dewanoumi	193:
38	Terukuni Manzo	1919/1977	Akita	173/161	Isegahama	193!
39	Maedayama Eigoro	1914/1971	Ehime	181/120	Takasago	192!
40	Azumafuji Kin'ichi	1921/1973	Tokyo-to	180/178	Takasago	193(
41	Chiyonoyama Masanobu	1926/1977	Hokkaido	191/131	Dewanoumi	1942
42	Kagamisato Kiyoji	1922/	Aomori	176/165	Tokitsukaze	194}
43	Yoshibayama Junnosuke	1920/1977	Hokkaido	179/161	Takashima	1938
44	Tochinishiki Kiyotaka	1925/	Tokyo-to	178/126	Kasugano	193!
45	Wakanohana Kanji	1928/	Aomori	179/105	Hanakago	194(
46	Asashio Taro	1929/	Kagoshima	189/145	Takasago	194{
47	Kashiwado Tsuyoshi	1938/	Yamagata	188/139	Isenoumi	195.
48	Taiho Koki	1940/	Hokkaido	187/153	Nishonoseki	195(
49	Tochinoumi Teruyoshi	1938/	Aomori	177/107	Kasugano	195!
50	Sadanoyama Shimmatsu	1938/	Nagasaki	182/122	Dewanoumi	195(
51	Tamanoumi Masahiro	1944/1971	Aichi	177/130	Kataonami	195!
52	Kitanofuji Katsuaki	1940/	Hokkaido	181/135	Kokonoe	195;
53	Kotozakura Masakatsu	1940/	Tottori	181/155	Sadogatake	195(
54	Wajima Hiroshi	1948/	Ishikawa	185/125	Hznakago	197(
55	Kitanoumi Toshimitsu	1953	Hokkaido	180/165	Mihogaseki	1967
56	Wakanohana Toshihito	1953/	Aomori	187/127	Futagoyama	1968
57	Mienoumi Tsuyoshi	1948/	Mie	181/130	Dewanoumi	1963
58	Chiyonofuji Mitsugu	1955/	Hokkaido	181/115	Kokonoe	1970
59	Takanosato Toshihide	1952/	Aomori	180/144	Futagoyama	1968

YOKOZUNA

Promoted to Ozeki	Promoted to Yokozuna	Makuuchi Record: Wins	Losses	Highest No. Successive Wins	Total Championships	Year Retired	Elder Name
1917	1922	192	94	7	2	1931	Shibatayama
1922	1923	134	60	14	1	1928	Asakayama
1920	1924	221	58	15	10	1930	Dewanoumi
1930	1932	308	92	27	9	†	Nishonoseki
1932	1935	174	69	13	1	1939	Shiranui**
1934	1936	247	136	16	2	1942	Minanogawa**
1937	1937	276	68	69	12	1945	Tokitsukaze
1940	1941	321	94	32	7	1953	Tatsunami
1941	1942	142	59	20	1	1946	Fujishima
1942	1942	271	91	17	2	1953	Isegahama
1938	1947	206	104	13	1	1949	Takasago
1945	1948	261	104	16	6	1954	Nishikido
1949	1951	366	149	17	6	1959	Kokonoe
1951	1953	360	163	17	4	1958	Tatsutagawa
1951	1954	304	151	15	1	1958	Miyagino
1953	1954	513	203	24	10	1960	Kasugano
1955	1958	546	235	24	10	1962	Futagoyama
1957	1959	431	248	12	5	1962	Takasago
1960	1961	599	240	15	5	1969	Kagamiyama
1960	1961	746	144	45	32	1971	Taiho
1962	1964	315	181	17	3	1966	Nakadachi
1962	1965	435	164	25	6	1968	Dewanoumi
1966	1970	469	221	19	6	†	
1966	1970	592	294	21	10	1974	Kokonoe
1967	1973	593	345	18	5	1974	Sadogatake
1972	1973	551	181	27	13	1981	Hanakago
1974	1974	951	350	22	24	1985	Kitanoumi
1977	1978	512	234	26	4	1983	Magaki
1975	1979					1980	Musashigawa
1981	1981						
1982	1983						

The New Kokugikan

The new Ryogoku Kokugikan, which opened in January 1985, blends modern materials and electronic convenience with traditional architectural forms. Built between April 1983 and December 1984, it cost fifteen billion yen (sixty million dollars) Although it holds the same number of spectators as its predecessor, about 11,000, it is much more spacious. New features are ramps and special seats for the handicapped, a few western-style boxes with chairs and tables around the perimeter of the first floor, rainwater storage and an energy-saving heat circulation system. The imperial box on the second-floor balcony is reached by a separate entrance.

For the first time all facilities have been brought together. The chaya are inside the entrance to the left, and the sumo museum and Japan Sumo Association offices are to the right. A sumo clinic is in the basement along with the archives, meeting rooms, rainwater storage tanks, and machinery. The training school has a practice area and a classroom in a second-floor rear extension.

The fact that the dohyo can be lowered into the basement, leaving a clear floor area for other activities, means that the sumo association can hire out the Kokugikan for cultural events such as concerts as well as sporting events.

The new Kokugikan is very near Ryogoku station on the Sobu line of the Japanese National Railways, and is also accessible by major highways.

Floor plan

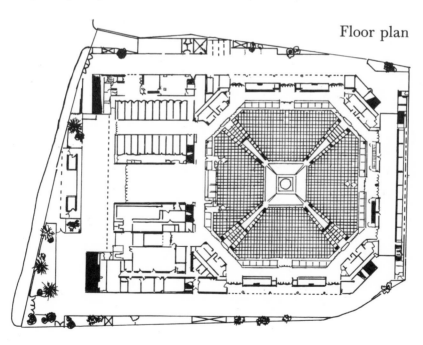

Section

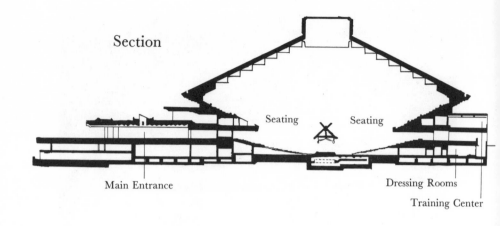

Seating   Seating

Main Entrance

Dressing Rooms

Training Center

Acknowledgments

I WISH TO EXPRESS my appreciation to the following people for their aid and encouragement during the course of the writing of this book: former Japan Sumo Association director Musashigawa Yoshihide and the staff of the Sumo Museum; Mizuno Naobumi, editor of the NHK Graph-published *Ozumo tokushugo* magazine; Kayama Iwane and the members of the Sumo no Tomo no Kai, especially Takahashi Maki and Konuma Seiichi; Kudo Akira of the Kudo Photography Studio in Ryogoku; photographer Kayama Takehiko; sportswriter Harada Hiroshi of the *Sankei News;* Yakuwa Mitsuharu, proprietor of the Koseisha bookstore in Kuramae; Professor Tsurumi Kazuko of Sophia University; Professor Ando Seiichi of Wakayama University; Professor Martin Colcutt, Professor Marius Jansen, Hasuike Reiko, and Andrew Loh of Princeton University; and my editor, Jim Conte. Gottsuan desu.

I would like to thank the following for allowing me to photograph objects from their collections to use as illustrative material. The number is that of the illustration in the book.

Sumo Museum: 1, 2, 3, 4, 5, 6, 8, 9, 10, 11, 12, 13, 17, 18, 19, 20, 22, 24, 25, 27, 28, 29, 31, 32, 35.

Kayama I.: 14, 15, 16, 21, 23, 26, 30, 34, 36, 37.

I also appreciate those who provided me with other photographs:
Kudo Photography Studio: 33, 38, 40, 41, 42, 43, 45, 47, 48, 49
NHK: 39, 44, 50, 52
Sankei Sports: 51
Justin B. Clairo: 7.

Credit for the contemporary photographs should be given to:
Jan Corash: 55, 58, 59, 60, 61
Ian Buruma: 56, 62, 63, 65
Sankei Photo Service: 53, 54, 57, 64

The illustrations on pages 190–91 are by Miho Miyazaki.

Mr. Abe Kozo of *Fuji Evening News* was especially helpful in the preparation of the revised edition.

Notes

INTRODUCTION

[1]Frances L. Hawkes, *Narrative of the Expedition of an American Squadron to the China Seas and Japan* (Washington, D.C.: Senate Printer, 1856), chapter XX.

[2]Arthur Walworth, *Black Ships Off Japan* (Hamden, Connecticut: Archeon Books, 1966), p. 200.

CHAPTER 1

[1]All Chinese sources quoted in this chapter are taken from the *Zhongguo tiyushi cankao ziliao* [Source Materials on Chinese Sports] (Peking: Renmin Tiyu Chubanshe, 1958), vol. 4, p. 31 ff.

[2]These theories are the work of such scholars as Yamakami Izumo and Wakamori Taro.

[3]The following description of crow sumo is taken from Yama-kami Izumo, *Shinwa no gensho* [The Phenomena of Mythology], Minzoku mingei sosho, vol. 36 (Tokyo: Iwasaki Bijutsusha, 19-69).

[4]*Ibid.*

[5]*Ibid.*

CHAPTER 2

[1]Heian-period poem quoted in Yokoyama Kendo, *Nihon sumo shi* [The History of Japanese Sumo] (Tokyo: Fuzambo, 1943), p. 16.

[2]*Ibid.*, p. 49.

[3]*Ibid.*, pp. 45–48.

CHAPTER 3

[1]Quoted in Ikeda Masao, editor, *Kokugi sumo no rekishi* [The History of Sumo, the National Sport] (Tokyo: Baseball Magazine Company, 1977), p. 144.

²Yokoyama, p. 59.

³*Ibid.*, pp. 58–59.

⁴*Ibid.*, p. 85.

⁵*Ibid.*, p. 85.

⁶*Ibid.*, p. 86.

⁷*Ibid.*, 152.

⁸Quoted in Furukawa Miki, *Edo jidai ozumo* [Grand Sumo in the Edo Period] (Tokyo: Yusankaku Publishing Co., 1969), pp. 377–78.

CHAPTER 4

¹*New York Times*, 29 September 1907, part 2, 4:4.

²*New York Times*, 12 November 1907, 1:5.

Selected Bibliography

ENGLISH SOURCES

"Art of Wrestling, The." *The Sun Trade Journal.* Vol. 8, numbers 11 and 12 (1902).

Aston, W. G., trans. *Nihongi: Chronicles of Japan from the Earliest Times to A.D. 697.* 1972. Rutland and Tokyo: Charles E. Tuttle Co.

Casal, U. A. *The Five Sacred Festivals of Ancient Japan.* Rutland and Tokyo: Sophia University and Charles E. Tuttle Co.

Draeger, Donn F. and Smith, Robert W. *Asian Fighting Arts.* 1968. Palo Alto and Tokyo: Kodansha International, Ltd.

Hikoyama, Kozo. *Sumo: Japanese Wrestling.* 1940. Tourist Library No. 34. Tokyo: Board of Tourist Industry, Japan Government Railways.

Kenrick, Doug. *The Book of Sumo: Sport, Spectacle, and Ritual.* 1969. New York and Tokyo: Walker/Weatherhill.

Newton, Clyde. *Makuuchi Rikishi of the Showa Period.* 1982. Privately printed.

Philippi, Donald L., trans. *Kojiki.* 1968. Tokyo: Princeton University Press/University of Tokyo Press.

Wheeler, John, with Kuhaulua, Jesse. *Takamiyama: The World of Sumo.* 1973. New York and Tokyo: Kodansha International, Ltd.

CHINESE AND JAPANESE SOURCES

Furukawa, Miki. *Edo jidai ozumo* [Grand Sumo in the Edo Period]. 1968. Tokyo: Yusankaku.

Ikeda, Masao, ed. *Kokugi sumo no rekishi* [The History of Sumo, the National Sport]. 1977. Tokyo: Baseball Magazine Co.

————. *Kokugi sumo no subete* [Everything About Sumo, the National Sport]. 1974. Tokyo: Baseball Magazine Co.

————. *Sumo hyakunen no rekishi* [Hundred-Year History of Sumo]. 1975. Tokyo: Kodansha.

————. *Sumo ukiyoe* [Ukiyoe Woodblock Prints of Sumo]. 1975. Tokyo: Baseball Magazine Co.

Minzoku no jiten [Dictionary of Folk Customs]. 1972. Tokyo: Iwasaki Bijutsusha.

Takanaga, Takehashi. *Sumo Showa shi gekido no gojunen* [The Showa Fifty-Year History of Events in Sumo]. 1975. Tokyo: Kobunsha.

Wakamori, Taro. *Asobi no bunkashi* [A Cultural History of Leisure]. 1973. Tokyo: Nihon Kotsukosha.

————. *Minzoku saijiki* [Folklore Almanac]. Minzoku mingei sosho [Folk Custom and Folk Art Series]: vol. 50. 1950. Tokyo: Iwasaki Bijutsusha.

————. *Nihon Fuzokushi* [A History of Japanese Customs]. Vols. 1–3. 1951. Tokyo: Yuhikaku.

————. *Rekishi: Densho no fudo* [History: The Adaptation of Legends]. 1971. Tokyo: Shinjimbutsu Oraisha.

————. *Sumo ima mukashi* [Sumo, Past and Present]. 1963. Tokyo Kawade Shobo.

Yamakami, Izumo. *Shinwa no gensho* [The Phenomena of Mythology]. 1969. Vol. 36. Tokyo: Iwasaki Bijutsusha.

Yokoyama, Kendo. *Nihon sumo shi* [The History of Japan's Sumo]. 1943. Tokyo: Fuzambo.

Zhongguo tiyushi cankao ziliao [Source Materials on Chinese Sports]. 1958. Vol. 4. Peking: Renmin Tiyu Chubanshe.

Index

221